Intuition

Saved My Life

Christine Gold

ISBN: 9798520203643

DEDICATION

I dedicate this to all the Empaths, sensitives, and light-workers in the world! Know that if you have life, you have a purpose! Keep shining! To my mom Teresa who passed April 29th, 2021. She was the epitome of selflessness, unconditional love, and kindness. To my boys, Connor & Keifer, to my sisters Colleen, Robyn, I love you. To my dad, I'm happy you're back in my life. My mentors, past and present, my journey would not be complete without your dedication and willingness to show up.

In each chapter, I will share reflections, a bit of SOUL work, and you will experience your inner transformation, aha, or epiphany. Please have fun, be open, and have the curiosity of a child.

CONTENTS

ACKNOWLEDGMENTS

I first and foremost acknowledge God; God is not a thing or a person; God is not a religion, but a state of consciousness, feeling, knowing, and divinity within us all.

1
CHAOS

Chaos is the tornado of living life of what you were told, shown, labeled, and witnessed. How can one see clearly or with vision when there's crap flying everywhere? Your job, your kids, your family, your addictions, your fear, your ego, your depression, your anxiety, your to-do list, your friends, your boss, your coworkers. It's no wonder there's chaos. There's no "you" in any of it!

Where was this behavior learned? Was it imprinted or stamped on you inside or outside of the womb? Who decided this? When was this karmic debt laid upon you? Did you ask for this without asking? Was this in your DNA somehow? You make choices every day, what to wear, what to eat, when to wake up or go to bed. Do I take this route or this one? Do I put in a solid 8 hours or 6? Do I go for drinks after work? Do I include some "me" time? Where is the self-care of exercise, rituals, and routine? Do I eat healthily or not? Do I go to bed on time or stay up late watching TV? I didn't see a lot of honoring of self (internal); I saw a ton of external and escapism crap, societal cues & habitual habits of a zombie. One who is "asleep" with no mind or a monkey mind? You're detached or attached, black or white; there is no grey, no stellar gateway to nirvana. Note to self; this is not self honoring but dishonor.

God made you perfectly. Somewhere along the way, you were told/blamed/shamed/molded or scolded that you were not. My life seems to operate from chaos, and I learned early in my life that it was normal. But what is normal anyway? To me, that's a label or a box. The only one who loves a box is a cat or a child. My mother had many jobs, sometimes three at a time. Things were always changing; she ran a dayhome as well. So, there were always kids around, never any peace and quiet. Maybe that's why I love it now; I crave it. Our world has gotten so busy with work, hobbies, commutes, and family. No wonder we feel we are operating at level chaos. It feels exhilarating to get on the ride. It feels right at the moment because everyone else is doing it, but once on, it's hard and scary to get off. That's your ego talking you into and out of getting off the chaos train. What is Ego? It's what keeps you stuck in chaos, shame, worry, doubt, blame, and fear.

My mom didn't have the best life growing up. From being a foster kid of 12, barely having enough food in the home, going to school without shoes, and being a ward of the government, she learned to operate from what she knew. All she knew was lack & scarcity, fear and worry, never having or being enough. Now I understand. I didn't before my spiritual awakening or leap into consciousness. Even now, sitting here as I write this, it's a very sad feeling. I have self-realization. I have empathy for my mom for the first time ever. So, in many ways, this book will be about healing for myself, my family, and my past lives to heal and seal the karmic contracts. I feel I'm operating from chaos sometimes, and I now know that is my ego taking me back to what I know, what I have always operated from, like it's a comfort thing, being comfortable is easy, going beyond your comfort is uncomfortable and takes strength, practice, courage, consistency, and determination. I know I have all those qualities. However, I tend to wobble depending on the situation, my mood, and what's happening around me at the time. So, I tend to lead with my emotions. When you know who you are and how emotion is a feeling and is fleeting – that will serve you well. If you wear your heart on your sleeve, are an empath, and have had issues with addictions, mental illness, and low self-esteem, then that's a problem.

I tend to have all these grandiose ideas, put them on paper as a goal. I follow through with a few, get discouraged and give up. That's why I'm writing this book; I know I have this in me; I have shit to say; I have a story to tell. Just like you do, everyone has a story inside; everyone has a voice that must be 'heard. Speak your truth! I have a few goals; I want to help others with depression & anxiety through intuitive development. We are all intuitive; we all have clairvoyance (seeing/knowing) auras, a person's energy, and a person's vibes. We know when we feel good or not so good around others. I operate from unconditional love for everyone, including people that make me feel yucky. I always wish them love, light, and blessings and move on. I'm also an empath, meaning I feel all the feels, I wear my heart on my sleeve, I love being of service to others (to my detriment sometimes, as others tend to take advantage of me and sap my energy – those are narcissists). I'm also about energy; every thought, every word you speak or write affects you and others. When your self-belief is low, it shows like a big rubber stamp on your forehead saying, "take advantage of me," "I'm desperate for attention," "I have no self-worth," "my time isn't valuable," and "I'm not important." That goes back to unhealed trauma from childhood or a recent, triggered repeating trauma. If your chakra, your meridian energy, is low/blocked/dirty/unbalanced or overactive, then it shows up as well. It throws your whole body out of whack, your mind is cluttered, your body is failing you, your emotional wellbeing is fragmented, and your spiritual being is operating from an ego-based level.

By all accounts, you're operating from such a low, dark and desperate level. It's like you have a spotlight on you for narcissists to see you from miles away like you send out a homing signal or GPS for them to find you & suck the little bit of life energy you have left. I find mediation is 50% of the battle of your monkey mind, your reptilian mind, the negative Nancy or Ned. If you can let go of the shit, float, be quiet for at least 30 minutes a day, and reprogram your thoughts/beliefs/systems that are in place. This takes practice, commitment, and part of your daily routine, sometimes multiple times a day. You will notice big changes, small incrementally, still leaps and strides. In your mind lies untapped strength, power and courage, and creativity. The art of being still and mindful is an art, a practice, and you will find so much of yourself in there and your lost self. I found myself through meditation, through struggling to let go of my ego, that's the shadow self, that part you still embrace, it's a part of who you are. Your ego made you safe and comfortable in your misery; your loathing, your negativity, your addictions, your traumas are your triggers. Unhealed trauma comes out in many different ways, making choices out of fear, scattered thoughts, and cloudy thinking. Depression is living in the past. Anxiety is living in the future. Then there's PTSD, S.A.D (Seasonal affective disorder), Panic attacks, and more. At this rate, I will take ten years to write a book because I allow my attachment to ego get the best of me. I'm trying to let go that I'm attached to anything or anyone.

The world makes it known that to be successful, you must have a great paying job, have a fabulous vehicle, great credit, wonderful clothes, toys, vacations, family, relationships, retirement fund savings, etc. I'm $601 a month away from losing what I perceive to be freedom, a vehicle. It's merely an object, a mode of transport to get around. So why am I attached to this, like it's a status symbol like I would be judged for saying I don't have a vehicle? This is absolute garbage! I'm talking about letting go of old beliefs, old stories, old patterns, old routines. It's time to shake things up energetically. Jump up and down, dance, shake your hands, and shake your butt; whatever it takes to get that sticky crap off, change your perspective. Take yourself out of your self-imposed prison of worry/guilt/shame/blame/fear/doubt. How does this start? Family programming 0-7 years of age, family beliefs (victims of victims), the school system (a big one for me, I felt I didn't belong there, I didn't belong anywhere). TV/media (mainly negative, low vibe energy), online/ads/billboards (look at us, the ego, you must have this), society in general (that small talk about the weather, the neighbors, gossip, etc.). Sociality in society, your experiences in life (How I was bullied in school, shamed by teachers, got my period in 7th grade while wearing white shorts — so embarrassing! The list goes on, so many things!) It was like I had PTSD. I was always feeling traumatized, still am to this day. I feel triggered; it's ridiculous!

Start new daily habits (be present, in the now, not living in the past or worrying about the future). Come home to self, make peace with self. Faulty beliefs of self; attract shitty people, friends, jobs, bosses, relationships, lack, and scarcity. Ruminating on things that are bad? Does any of this sound familiar? 90% of the developed world lives like this! Focus on what makes us feel good, not bad! I was broke and broken, intense pain and suffering. I cried buckets/oceans of tears. Now I want to transmute my pain into power & love. Letting go of lower vibration emotions, it's like we are hardwired for suffering and feeling bad! Low vibes include those emotions guilt/shame/blame etc. and alcohol/drugs/food/gossip/jealousy/comparison

Instead, focus on God, high vibe emotions, watch babies & children, animals, gratitude, someone you love, Yoga, meditation, hypnotherapy, EFT/tapping, counseling, nature, breathing properly (many of us hold our breath because we're anxious, let it go!) Qi-gong/Wim Hof will help with your breathing/breathwork. Use the breath to soothe ourselves, calm, lead us to the place with no thought and bliss. For me, it's found in writing, journaling, letting go & go within. Then there's the inner child work, go back and speak to your younger self. Tell that child it's okay; you're loved, you're safe, you're accepted, you're amazing, you're worthy, I believe in you, we love you, give lots of hugs and sit with that child until you have a sense of connection again. Carry a picture of your younger self, especially when choosing shitty people/food/drugs/addictions.

Talk to them and find out why & that it's okay, you don't need to do that, you are enough just the way you are. If we don't love ourselves, we choose things that are not our highest! Lack of self-love and suffering keeps you in that self-imposed prison! Then there's diet, weight, something I struggled with since I was a child. 90% of what goes into your gut is linked to serotonin development, so the cleaner/fresher/healthier/high vibe it is, the better your mood will be! Then it's cyclical, and you will crave the healthy stuff and reject the low vibe stuff, the body remembers. *The quality of my life with myself depends on the conversation I have with myself.* Monitor your emotions of self and others. Live and be present, don't go to the past or the future; that's where depression and anxiety live. Find out the root cause of your emotions, thoughts, and how you speak to yourself. Let yourself know it's safe; it's okay! Active programming, I believe in you, I am worthy, I am enough, I am love, light, deserving, and I am powerful. Do this daily, tell yourself these things and more. I believe in you! That will program into the subconscious/change/reprogram the mind! Quality of sleep is important; 50% of people suffer from insomnia! Plan and prepare your sleep, dark, and cool room, no TV, no screens or phones, no eating 4-5 hours before bed, earplugs, essential oils, prayer, reading, put on delta wave music to help with your brain waves, positive self-talk, give yourself permission to let go, it's safe, and I am enough!

Stop the comparison; stop judging how good you are by how much money you make; what a crock of shit! It's a farce; it's a lie; it's programming! Love yourself! Come home to self and identity. Know what your faulty beliefs are, become awake, stop unhealthy patterns, and step out of your unawakening dream. Reprogram faulty beliefs, find out where/who you truly are, learn how to love yourself. Forgive yourself and others, including family/friends/coworkers/bosses, etc., whoever wronged or hurt you. Many of you treat yourself badly with relationships, money, jobs, etc. It's not your fault; we all make mistakes! Teenagers who have a home, all the food they could want to feed them for the rest of their life, money, jobs, cars, toys, etc., and yet still unhappy and suicidal. Suicide amongst teens is the 2nd leading cause of death! That's wrong; that's broken. We need to unravel this, heal this before it becomes a stat for tweens or younger! Life is not about how much you accumulate. Have you ever seen a Hurst with a U-Haul attached to it? I haven't! We don't take our shit, our belongings, and our money with us!?! *Stop judging the success of your life based on your bank account!* Don't be tied to the digits; the government is printing money; they are basically bankrupt! Gold isn't even tied to our money anymore. It's a separate commodity. I used to think about what I made, how much money I had, my title or position in a company, my cars, and my clothes.

My stuff is who I AM – my soul, what makes me a bigger or better person. Like my sister says, she did some soul mapping and found that our family lineage hides or has an inferiority complex. Meaning we act like we are so grandiose, better than everybody, or act like I'm more important, to have all this stuff, these titles that somehow makes me important, be seen, be recognized – I see now that it comes from my childhood and made me feel small, to hide, that I didn't matter. I was a bother, and I was annoying or a hassle by my mom, who was super stressed, overworked, struggling with some sort of mental health issues and unhealed childhood trauma. I'm struggling to write this book, to commit the time and the presence to do so. Although writing a book is always on my mind, in my forefront, I have committed 1 hour every day to write around 500 words at a time. This honors my true self, the self that wants to come out and help others through healing myself. I will help at least one person. See, that small part of me thinks only one; why not think bigger and say, two people! Or is that my ego, wanting to be seen as helping others, so I look good, better, etc. "God's your only real parent anyways. You rest, you just rest." "God's voice speaks to me throughout the day." A Course in Miracles. Whatever feels right to you, I'm attracted to colors, songs, movies, poems, books, nature, animals, signs, symbols, and certain conversations. I look to everything in the universe to inspire me, always go to the light. There's a synergy & energy to foods that are higher vibration vs. lower vibration. Look to things that appeal to you, are you drawn to certain colors, foods, smells, what feeds your soul, what's your source of soul food, smile more, attracted to light (otherwise, you're a vampire).

What do you believe in? Do you believe in yourself, your dharma, your light, God, spirit, and more? I say start with you, go deep, and find out where are the dark pieces and bits are. What are the dark spaces you hold; shine light on them. Acknowledge it, work through it, get help if you're unsure how or where to start. Just start, notice what drains you, what inspires you, what lights you up, what takes you down? True freedom is a spiritual state of mind, a sense of independence. How can you if you don't know who you are? I am free! You are free! Look for the shiny parts of yourself, and you will feel lighter, feeling like your soul is being fed. So, you easily move toward that, move toward the light, your shifting dimensional frequencies from 3D to 5D — the stuff of this world 3D is heavy and dense. If you can get the feeling of light, you will raise your vibration, change your consciousness, dig into your subconscious; you cannot do this if you don't know who you are. Your light is equal to your true identity. Choosing to identify, who AM I? When we remember that morsel, how it tastes to our soul helps us see who we truly are. Given your circumstances, you should be miserable to other people choosing to drink the punch of this world, a whole other level of insanity. I'm saying dig deep to get to the tough stuff, and this requires courage to show up and get real. Real about whom you truly are, who you were always meant to be, somewhere along the way, you forgot; you were told; you were shamed; you were guilted; you were made to feel less than.

That's an unhealed trauma, a trauma that's worth uncovering, opening up, finding out where it comes from, forgive them and yourself, send love to it, and release it. If you have to, do these multiple times as it shows up again, it's there to show you something needs addressing, not dismissing. Love is often more invisible, and life is more shallow. Grab it and uncover where it comes from, rinse and repeat until you no longer feel it, or triggered or going/living in low vibes or doing things that are not you! Boundary setting is an advanced spiritual concept, and people will start to sense what you're about, then they know what they can and cannot get from you. Be a rod of light, your center, your kundalini, that staff, that light. It supports me, my inner support, and my guide. You're not clean and sober yet. I'm working at it, live in the light, not lying, not cheating, and living in your principles/morals — when all of a sudden, it's not an option. Learning to say no to the things that don't resonate with spirit, light, and with God. Don't feed into the lies of the world. Own your sense of who you are. I AM as God created me, and I have no interest in anything else. I'm not still fighting my fears; I'm there, I'm free, it doesn't matter, there's no other option. That's spiritual freedom. Having an addiction is a false sense of freedom. That involves responsibility, getting to know yourself, and nurturing your soul. People forget how, the quick out, winning arguments, can't wait to die (no more pain/disease). Even death is a false form of independence because, on the other side, anything unhealed emotionally comes back in your other life/reincarnation.

I'm trying to change the vibe of the world, to stop people from drinking from the punch of the world. Find your light, yourself, your unconditional love. You're fighting the good fight, even dying knowing that you tried your best with the light, become an example for everyone else. Believe in who you are, believe in you, Be You! People are fighting themselves more than they realize. It's always someone else (media, neighbors, family, etc.). Viruses will treat you like Velcro, unhealed cells like untreated trauma/wounds. Ego is running the show, or are you running? I believe ego runs many of our lives as a program. Like a routine, time to shake up the routine. Isn't it time to try something different, see things with new eyes, not skewed eyes? I fell off the treadmill exhausted, tired of chasing the preverbal golden carrot. Was it golden, or was it a reflection of the illusion I so desperately wanted to see? So many questions, that's when the real soul's purpose and the journey starts.

Surrendering to the universe, waving the white flag, and saying, okay, I'm here! I'm exhausted and ready to listen, find the quiet white spaces in my mind's eye to finally see the divinity that is who we all are. The universe was waiting patiently, holding space for you when you realize there is no more space and the dark matter does matter; that's where you shine a light on it to be revealed.

So, I know this to be true. Chaos was a reverberation of the ego, the false narrative, the broken programming, the virus of the mind that tried to swallow the soul. It almost felt like hell, that image of all the lost souls reaching out from the flames, help me, help us! Yes, that was me; Responsibility tells me I created my hell. Now it's time for me to realize heaven on earth. That heaven was always waiting for me to realize fully with new eyes, new vision, one eye, third eye diving deep into myself at every angle. Truly that is an image I want to imagine and deep dive into the soul pool.

SOULWORK

Take the time to reflect, grab your journal and start to channel what comes through. What are your first thoughts, feelings, and visions? Don't overthink or guess; feel! That's intuition.

What does magic mean to you?

What are your dreams now? Dream big!

What were your dreams as a child?

What lights you up?

What are you passionate about?

Let's find your soul's purpose!

How do you take care of yourself at a 360-degree level?

(Mentally, Physically, Emotionally, Spiritually, Financially, and Relationships.)

2

LIVING IN FEAR

I was controlled by the frightened parts of my personality. It's not easy to say no to a drink when you're an alcoholic, food when you overeat, or that new outfit when you're a shopaholic, etc. My whole life, I learned that fear was a big motivator, what I operate from, what motivates me, what gives me and keeps my edge. I was living in a low vibration. At the time, I had no idea. I didn't know what that meant, what that looked like, how that felt. I used alcohol, sex, and cigarettes to mask, stuff, hold down and avoid my fear, worry, doubt, and unworthiness. I now know this is my family's ancestral history of inherent inferiority. *Inferior Definition — Feeling inferior means feeling inadequate or below others in terms of social, physical, intellectual, or psychological attributes. Inferiority Complex "Symptoms" or Low self-esteem is Social Withdrawal.*

People with inferiority complex usually feel uncomfortable being around others, particularly in a crowded place, fault finding, performance anxiety, craving for attention, increased sensitivity, and easily feeling disrespected. I feel that stemmed from always being the tall girl up until grade 9. I thought it was a curse and not a gift, add extra weight to the mix, and I felt like the Jolly green giant, except I wasn't so jolly. My dad left when I was 4, still, to this day, I don't know why, the whole story or real reason. I felt neglected, abandoned, and not good enough as I had limited interactions with my dad. I was a sad, mixed-up, angry and hurt little girl. I was that little girl who was looking for approval, belonging, and meaning wherever she went. I broadcast that shit out like it was the 5G network or wore the biggest button that said use me, abuse me, and throw me away. Many of my relationships were fleeting, one-night stands, abusive in some way, that all stemmed from me not liking who I was, that I was angry at the world, I was trying to fit in somewhere that would never fit in. I wasn't meant for this cookie-cutter world. I'm an individual, a soul, an energy that spreads its wings and soars!

I didn't know I had the power to open my wings, to untie my hands, to expand love into myself. Recognizing I was already a shining beacon of light within, I had to find the switch and turn it on. That took 44 years to find.

In my next life, I will have that switch activated upon entering the world. I will be the teacher, the guide, and the guru of unconditional love. Even as I write this, I can feel the energy, the love unconditionally pouring out through my fingertips and into the keystrokes. The reason I wanted to write this book is to help anyone who is stuck, lost, depressed, exhausted, negative, angry, frustrated, etc. To lead you to a place of healing, unconditional love, find your peace, your clarity, your joy, your dharma (your purpose), that's my reason for everyone. I realize I cannot help everyone, and some might even scoff at the idea. My ego is aware of that. One person who can be transformed or find transformation is one less person suffering in a world of suffering. The 3D world was meant to keep you down, keep your head down, heart down, fear up, worry up, materialism up, and addictions up. What I want is the opposite as the collective to find our source of connection again, find love, find joy, find our inner child, heal our traumas, addictions, hate, distrust, worry, and fear. Bring it back to love, soul remembrance, and the love that has always been there from the beginning. To heal that past family trauma line, cut the cords of attachment, and walk through it all with love unconditionally. Practice self-care daily to extend that to others and be the shining example of light.

How to heal from hurt, grief, and loss. This is achieved through loss of ego. Yes, your ego and mind will see it that way. Your soul, however, craves this separation from the control that ego has held over you for years. I also discovered validation is everything, to be heard by someone and learning to understand who we are! To be understood, heard, and validated is what every human being wants and needs for their soul. I love one of Brene Brown's quotes, love her books and research. She says, "Shame is the gateway to perfectionism." Perfectionists live in shame. Shame derives its power from being unspeakable. We judge people in areas where we're vulnerable to shame. Vulnerability led to anxiety, which led to shame, which led to disconnection, which led to addictions to food/sex/alcohol.

Empathy is the antidote to shame, empathy with self and others. We are hardwired for connection. 80 to 85% of the population is on some sort of drug (alcohol/prescription/food). The way we grow our food is full of chemicals. 90% of us are full of chemicals. We are numbing ourselves with crap, and I choose to sharpen my skills, my intuition, my knowing's, and myself. Your intelligence has betrayed you, and there is no stable base, so your intelligence works against you. Your thoughts belong to you, or you belong to your thoughts — choose wisely. Happiness is generated within. What comes within you must be the way you want it. If it's outside of you, you cannot control it. Do you want your mind controlled, or do you want it liberated? Intelligence is not a serious problem; it's a blessing. You have intelligence for which you do not have a stable enough platform.

We need more physicality, nature, connection with body, mind, and spirit. Lining up and aligning your geometry with the cosmic geometry to be congruent. Get up between 3:30 am to 3:40 am. Your body is naturally awake at that time, which is a very spiritual time. Many of us wake up at that time but don't realize it. If it takes 12 years of schooling to learn everything about the world, why do you need a quick hit, quick mantra, quick reading, whatever it is? Is your life not worth investing in as well? One mantra will not change your life. It takes time, commitment, energy, focus, and practice, repeated practice day in & day out. Yes, I have struggled with the routine of a gratitude journal, dream journal, yoga, grounding, chakra balancing, healthy eating, reading, etc. You don't think it's hard, gets routine and boring, maybe we think it's hard? If I ever feel that way, listen to what the body wants, what's going on around you? Even as I'm writing this, I feel as though I'm an imposter, like who Am I to give you advice? See, that's how the ego works, always wanting to keep you down, in a negative frame of mind, like somehow, you're unworthy. Well, that's a bunch of bullshit; you are unique, you are love, you are light, you are here for a reason, you are here for an important thing, and you just don't know it yet. You haven't given yourself the time or space to do so. So, I invite you to do so, to explore, to play, to find out what brings you joy and what doesn't! Play more, feel more, just be.

I feel quite fortunate to have an army of angels, guides, and loved ones behind me. Let me tell you all of the stupid things I have done, gotten into, and I'm sure the times I might have died or had close calls. You know for damn sure that there's a reason I'm writing this book, why I'm doing videos online through Facebook or YouTube. I feel like I'm the female version of Wayne Dyer. He is a founding father of the ego, how it's your dark side, your shadow self, and how society has made the ego the forefront of our lives. That it's normal to operate from, to be in, to think what you do for a living is who you are. That the clothing, the car, the money, that bank account, and the retirement fund is what makes you who you are. I'm here to tell you that's the ego. That's not who we are spiritually. We are spiritual beings; we are here to help each other, connect, and collaborate, grow, and be present in a world that has checked out, eyes glazed/glossed over, and operating from robot mode. Do you ever see the robots? They are all around you. Your friends, family, coworkers, they are everywhere. They put on the mask of "look at me." "I'm so happy buying these things because somehow this will make me a better person." Those things are here to keep you down, depressed, anxious, numb, drugged up to keep your eyes on the proverbial happiness golden ticket. That's not happiness; that's death. Slowly but surely, it will put you in the ground faster than anything else. Ever heard of the term, living longer, dying slowly? I want to live slowly and die longer. I know both sound wrong, is it really?

Depending on your perspective, perspective requires us to slow down, sit in silence, unplug from everything that distracts us and plugs into what allows us to expand, be present, be awake, and be fully aware conscious. That consciousness is a beautiful thing. That thing is your heart chakra, once it's fully replenished from years of auto programming or autopilot. Your heart operates from the inner compass. That compass was broken while being asleep or robot-like. It's time to fully delve into the unknown, the darker parts of yourself, your soul to find out what's really there. What keeps you fully awake, coherent, intelligent, and not misguided, misdirected, in the ego, being like the joneses? It's not easy to do. If it were, everyone would do it. It requires faith, and it requires bravery. It requires going it alone as many will think you are crazy, weird, or not part of the club (I've been to the club, and it's overrated and draining!). I'm telling you to get yourself right. Your next life and next lifetime will be amazing, and no more struggle for you. Your ancestral family will thank and love you for it. I promise. I have been struggling with myself and my ego; I feel the energy shifts, especially with the moon energy. I feel I'm trying to be everything for everyone, and I'm trying to do everything. I feel the scattered energies. There are many things going on, and I feel like I was separate from GOD — "when GOD is within me." *"What we are is love, and all we have to do is be that," Lao Zhu*

Ego is trying to break me; my subconsciousness is roaring up again, like the lion, like the false idol, false self. I have had my struggles, mainly about worth. Again, I feel it's an inherent belief about me, passed down through the generations. We're talking thousands of years to infinity — to the beginning of time and space. That is how strongly I feel about this. It's my duty to heal the family bloodlines/heritage/karma/shadows/contracts, etc. I even have trouble writing this book, I have no trouble bragging to others about how I'm writing a book and this and that, but I'm not committed to daily writing. Is it because of my worth? Do I feel ashamed or guilty because there's a certain way to do it or not to do it or write it? Am I supposed to have 500 words every day, or is it 1,000? Is this my ego talking and taking over? All these roadblocks and hurdles or the loop of shoulda, woulda, coulda. So free to offer advice or control but nothing regarding inspiration, guidance, unconditional love, and love some more. It has been weeks since I wrote a chapter, not sure why. I guess I thought, or my ego thought I didn't matter, I don't deserve to write a book, who do I think I AM? That inherent unworthiness is a family trait, and I learned growing up that I was to be seen and not heard, that I was a bother, a pain in the ass, I cost money, I have no money because of you, you cost too much, you eat too much, you cry too much, you're fat, you're too tall, you're too pretty, you're ugly, you're fat, Chrissy pissy — I mean, the shame and bullying went on for years. I took that and created a persona, a mask to be someone I wasn't, but other people liked me, they really liked me, so sad! This is sad, people are narcissists, and I attracted them.

Like moths to a flame, they could see the hurt, the belonging, the unworthiness all over me like a badge or a beacon — come hurt me because I'm desperate for attention and someone to like me. I'm still doing this in my business. I'm a medium, I read for people, I help heal people with messages from spirits, angels, guides, and loved ones who have crossed over — I also do Reiki and healings. I always feel wonderful after each reading or healing with a client, and I feel like I'm floating on cloud nine or chakra 55, or is it 144? Where do I start? The journey is a long, winding path with no shortcuts because you will find yourself in the same spot. I still live in fear sometimes, but I catch myself faster these days. That's partly because I'm conscious, aware, more in tune with my body, my emotions through meditation & yoga mainly, some deep breathing, and Reiki.

SOULWORK

We dive into your fears, your blocks, your trauma, your inner child healing, and your ego!

What are your fears? What keeps you up at night?

What is keeping you from your magic?

Where did these fears and blocks come from?

Trauma, and addictions, and triggers.

Inner child?

Ego? Judgment, worry, overwhelm, negativity, status, money, anxiety, blame, shame, unworthiness, busyness, avoidance, and numbing.

3

WORTH

Worthiness or worth is defined as "good or suitable enough" there were other definitions, but this one stood out for me, as it relates to a person more than recognition or material item/reward/award. I'm thinking good and suitable enough for whom? Then it hits me as I write this, a freaky aha moment: for society, for others, your mother, your brother, your boss, your friends, etc. Nowhere is there a piece about how your worth is more valuable and intrinsically part of your soul. You define the worth, not your ego, either. You are already worthy, always have been, always will be. You were born worthy, perfectly, gifted and beautiful. Where did you lose your worth? Did things chip away at it bit by bit? Did it get buried by trauma, by fear, by addictions, by avoidance? By numbing?

How do you reclaim your worth? I started with one, with myself. Stripping away all the layers of who I thought I was and revealed a little girl who was always too shy, always too scared, always too loud, always too emotional. I was always too tall, too chubby, too pretty (whatever that means), and more. I found with each label or statement of myself, and I realized that those were other people's projections put on me. Their mirrors of what they were missing reflected onto me. Little did I know, I was a magnifying glass, a mere reflection of what was wounded in them, triggered in them was in me. Little did we know that it was a shining, beaming, brilliant, white light. That light is blinding their eyes, shocking at first, releasing shadows that needed to be released. We are to be seen, and no more hiding. Then it all unleashed; we saw each other for the first time. There was no flaw, no defect, and no unworthiness to begin with. That was the illusion, the masking of our true divinity. I never realized it at that moment. I attracted all the darkness because I, too, was darkness. I attracted the narcissistic relationships because I had narcissistic tendencies knowingly or unknowingly.

It takes self-realization and full responsibility to come to this. I didn't know my worth; they also didn't know it as well. I didn't know what was happening, and I thought I was losing my mind, going crazy, not good enough, a bad girl who didn't deserve love or anything good in her life. If I did, it was sheer luck, or it was a co-incidence. That was my faulty thinking, my ego was so full of itself, and it let me believe this for so many years. When you finally see it crashing down, then energetically you become brighter, lighter, you begin to fill yourself up with love, with light, with hope, with all the things you were born into this world with. Yes, I'm being honest here. Writing this five years ago would make my eyes roll. Now I know this is who I have unraveled to become. I'm stepping into my sovereign heart space with grace. I'm full of joy, peace, abundance, and truth. The truth magnifies the love; it's a truly cyclical feeling. The more we practice that feeling, the more we step into our being.

The so-called "temple of Christine" has collapsed, reminding me of the Golden Buddha story. Golden Buddha, or the Pra Buddha Mahasuwan Patimakon. Located in Wat Traimit, a temple in Bangkok, the Golden Buddha is about five and a half tons of solid gold. Pious Buddhists describe this statue as reflecting the true nature of the Buddha, and visitors from all over the world come to marvel at the beauty of this ancient treasure. The village was going to be invaded, so they covered the Golden Buddha in concrete to hide the "treasure," years passed, and everyone forgot about the gold. Until a new leader ordered the Buddha to be moved, when they went to move it, some concrete fell off and revealed the Golden Buddha's hidden treasure.

To reveal what was perceived as forgotten, the remembrance of whom we are, the treasure. I can start over again, learning, growing, sharing, teaching, and expanding/integrating into my utmost light body being of light that was born into this world 45 years ago. We are all beings of brilliant white light, crystalline to mother earth, to God, to the divine mother, and beyond the cosmos and universe. Worthiness, by any definition, is you! Knowing it inherently takes time, practice, acknowledgment, and courage. The courage to get a big head or being full of yourself, the right balance of confidence and knowing. That's my definition. That came from what I tell my clients' practice — rinse — repeat! I mean, we all have to practice something if we want to excel at something. Excel doesn't mean perfect or straight A's either. That is an Ego thing. Excel by having fun, trying something new or scary, and finding out what you're made of. You will be surprised, pleasantly surprised! Then you start to build yourself up. Reminds me of a song as I write this. Build me up, buttercup baby, just to let me down. Now how does that happen? By giving up, being too critical and perfect! So, don't be a downer on yourself; get down and have fun with yourself. That is character and confidence building. So put your heart, soul, and magic into a project or a cause. Maybe the cause is you because you forgot about yourself along the way trying to prove your worth. When truly you already were worthy, always! Then you take that worthiness project called self-realized and share it with others. Watch how they transform in front of you, watch their first epiphanies and aha moments.

The sheer giddiness of excitement; when they make a connection to their worth. That feeling transcends, uplifts, motivates, and vibrates out to the world. So really, you are healing others without having to have special training or certification or a title. That cannot be measured here on earth but in the heart. Worth comes from the healing work, the radical acceptance of yourself and your flaws. Funny, I'm still using and hearing the word flaw. We are not flawed. Rather, we have a belief system. That BS "Belief System" exists to be transcended. We think we are not perfect in the matrix or 3D world. However, I know we are already perfect in the universe and with God. That is all that matters! I recall a story about a woman who was on Alan Cohen's weekly coaching calls on Zoom. She was having trouble accepting her perceived imperfections, trying to get everything perfect and be perfect. Alan replied with a twinkle in his ocean blue eyes, "The Imperfectionist sees the flaws in everything, rather a perfectionist is already perfect, and there is no imperfection."

SOULWORK

This is a short chapter on worth, I believe you are already on your worthiness journey. So with that in mind, let's work on Mantra's (A sacred verbal formula repeated in prayer, meditation, or incantation, such as an invocation of a god, magic, or a syllable or portion of scripture containing mystical potentialities). Affirmation (Affirmations are dynamic and practical — not wishful thinking) and Decree (to speak of God's eternal wisdom and plan for creation).

With that in mind, think of words filled with love that lift you up and inspire you. Such words include Love, kindness, worth, peace, joy, beauty, magical, abundance etc. Search for the feeling you are trying to emote or build up. If you lack self-esteem, you can start by saying "I am deeply grateful for my body, my health, and my unique talents."

Start with one word, put them on sticky notes all over your home, your car, your computer. Record them on your phone, write them out and speak them into being.

The more you practice filling up with the good, the more your soul will recognize this as your natural state of being. That practice will manifest more and more abundance; it's a cyclical practice. Cycling in and cycling out, radiating out to the world!

4

MY STORY

Yes, I have been homeless, been on social assistance, and lived at a women's shelter. Had two abortions, been blackout drunk, been drugged, and raped. I have also escaped some situations that could have gone badly. I know I have an angelic team with me; their assignment is not for the faint of heart. I felt abandoned by my father (he left when I was 4, in and out of my life, up until the death of his sister). I feel my dad realizes just how much healing we all have to do to mend any relationship that needs mending, to say the things that need to be said so that an inner understanding and healing takes place.

My mother tried her best with the tools she had and was hated by my stepfather. My mom had a hard life, a child of the '50s & '60s, and I want to honor her as she passed on April 29th, 2021. My mom had a family, except the new husband didn't want her. So, she was placed in an orphanage and then into foster care with a family of 12. She never healed from the abandonment issues of never feeling like she fit in or was truly accepted or wanted. That wound transcended into my sister and me. She was also assaulted. I'm sure there was some abuse too. Bless her heart; she has the biggest heart, always helping where she could. She would take in all sorts, from kids to animals. She had spunk and didn't mince words when someone crossed her. Highly intuitive, too, although we never talked about it. Her unhealed trauma was masked by alcohol. I remember when she would call me up; sometimes, I would dread having to talk to her. I could always tell if she had been drinking. It was heart-wrenching, and I asked her to get help, talk to someone. I know in the end, we have to make that choice for ourselves, no one else. I needed to get off my soapbox and just meet her at her beautiful childlike soulful self. Knowing she is perfection in every sense. I do that every night in my dreams or when I'm out in nature, my favorite place to be. She is in the trees, the birds, hummingbirds especially, the flowers, all of it! Please hug your mom, parents, and kids, whoever you love, tell them, show them, and don't have any regrets or guilt when they pass. Know that you loved, honored, and cherished them. All I know is she made her mark in the world, such a beautiful impression.

I have left relationships with nothing except the shirt on my back. Except I was always accused by my ex-boyfriends as being a gold digger, that I wanted to take all of their money and possessions when I left. I later realized that was their shit, not mine. Being an empath, it took many years to figure this out. Being an empath, we take on every word, every trauma, and every energy as our own. Like it's our stuff, pretty soon it's like carrying the weight of an extra person. It weighs on you, it weighs you down, and it crushes your very spirit. Soon you begin to manifest diseases, illnesses, emotions, etc., from unhealed empathy absorption. It's distressing, so next time you want to unleash on someone. Think, is it kind, is it necessary, and is it true? I'm sure at some point, I, too, had narcissistic tendencies and behaviors. How can you not? Hanging around with people like that, eventually like when you start speaking with a British accent after staying in England for a while, is completely natural. So never feel bad; that's what they want you to feel. I get it. I feel you, I hear you, I see you, and I know you. I'm here to be with you while you are going through, as they say, the dark night of the soul. This is the part where ego and your soul self-merge. This is not an overnight sensation or a quick fix. This takes the hard work, the tough stuff, the being and feeling every emotion and trauma, going through the pain to come out all bright and shiny.

I love the flow of my story, how it unfolds itself day by day, minute by minute, second by second, year by year. The universe is gently guiding you or pushing you over the edge and off the beaten path. Walk to the beat of your drum, music, and song — we each have our inner symphony. We just need to be quiet long enough to hear the faint songs in your heart. The universe sends us all sorts of signs and symbols. I keep a book of this to have a brilliant conversation with my guides/angels and loved ones. In fact, we are sent signs through our dreams, songs, animals, repeating numbers, coins, lights flickering, electronics freezing or not working, smells, tastes, people (especially children!), and even billboards/pictures/books. Children and animals, especially as they are the purest form of unconditional love, have no ego, no programs, just love. They teach us how to love ourselves with no conditions, no rules, no inhibitions, just purity at its highest form. Dreams are a gateway to the other side, other dimensions, and other universes parallel to our 3D world. It's like Mother Earth holds the crystals, the crystalline grid energy where we ground and replenish ourselves. Mother Earth (Gaia) holds a space for us for unconditional love and healing. That crystalline grid is pure magic. The rainbow spectrum of infinite light raises us to new levels of a dimension beyond space, time, and its infinite. Dreams for me are a way to connect with my guides/angels/loved ones and travel earth years or days with the collective energy.

I get messages through my dreams that don't make sense, but after I write my nightly dreams in, I go back and read my week. Many times, I receive aha moments, epiphanies, and knowing's for myself and for my clients (When I have readings with clients 1-2 days prior — I astral travel, I see where they live, who they are, how they are, what they are feeling mentally/physically/emotionally & spiritually.). I astral travel with my son's Uncle, John. Although we have never met, we meet at a soul level. He has been my mentor, my guide, and his guides/angels/loved ones protect and travel with my collective energy. He is 82 and is a wizard, shaman, and healer. He has many years, lifetimes of knowledge, and I soak it all in! We also have dragons that travel with us in our dreams. They are our protectors, healers, and that beam of light that surrounds us wherever we go. Because

I say once you turn that inner light on, it never goes off. It's like it broadcasts it to the world, like Batman's bat signal. This can leave you open to attack from folks that are asleep, stuck in ego, and narcissists. As well, I was reflecting my wounds onto them and them onto me. I take responsibility too. I'm no longer the victim here. I'm merely explaining the beginner's mind, the empath's journey. They see it, they feel it, like a source of un-tapped energy for them to feel better or recharge. It's the moth to a flame analogy. It truly is! I have a soul's con-tract, something I understood and signed before coming to earth. I might not know what that is.

I'm living it every day and finding out along the way. That's my journey, my path, my evolution. I came here to heal what was unhealed in the past, intergenerational trauma. I feel I'm leading others by example, even though some days I don't want to lead. That's the infe-rior part of me that wants to hide and stay safe. That's why God, prayer, meditation, protection, grounding, af-firmations, wrapping, and seeing ourselves in balls/spheres of pure white light are so very important. These are tied to the crystalline energy, the spectrum. It radiates pure love and bounces off us and radiates into others, whether they feel it or not. It's like a beautiful rose between us, the shimmers of unconditional love and light beam back and forth between us — nothing escapes it. That's why some are triggered by us, like rattling the cage of their inner demons/traumas/hurts. Some will take it in and feel a sense of calm, peace, and relaxation. Some will absorb it and merge it into the dark parts of their shadow self. And some will use it as power and gaslighting for you and others. So, let the rattling continue in your soul until there is nothing left to rattle, shake, loose, or push. Know that in the healing journey, there will be triumphs, there will be tears; know that you were made for this time. Just like I was, I signed a soul's contract, even though I don't remember. Really, I do remember, I have moments of déjà vu, and I'm okay. I'm getting it.

SOULWORK

Dreams — Buy yourself a beautiful journal that reminds you of dreams and dreaming. Here you will start to write in this book each night if you can. It then becomes a practice, a ritual, a sacred signal to the universe. You may ask your guides, angels, and loved ones to come in and assist you. Any spirit animals, God, source, whatever you believe in to assist you.

You may say a prayer; whatever your intention is will come to fruition. Now it might take a few days or weeks for words, images, symbols to come forward in your dreams. Do not despair or agonize over it, be relaxed and know it will happen because when we let go, we surrender.

Please do not get attached to the dream either. Many times, it's not for us. Maybe we're not ready to hear the message yet. It will all make sense when you're ready.

5

SOULS PURPOSE

What do I mean by Soul's Purpose? I mean, every one of us has a soul, a blueprint, a calling that we were born with. We come into this world with inherent branding from God to impact the world, one person at a time. Each one of us has a unique ability to help guide others to their soul's purpose, and this is done through connection. We are here for connection, to bridge those connections. How do I know what my purpose is? It's a feeling, and it's a knowing. It just feels good, sometimes scary, sometimes unknown, and sometimes lonely. That's the path of your soul's purpose. You have the inner light to light the way for yourself and others.

My heart wants for you what I have unleashed, after 44 years, 44 years. It's not the age that matters; it's the decision you decided for yourself and your soul that your worthiness was never an issue. There is still time, and there is always time; it's never too late. You're not too old, too young, too tall, too short, not an expert, scared to death! I'm merely a humble servant of God. Yes, I used the G or J word (Jesus). I don't understand why there is such a strong attachment to Christianity — maybe the decades of wars/fighting/gaslighting/tyranny of religion in general. Many do not understand; they only form and gather their experiences and perceptions of what religion was to them. Many live in fear and judgment, and many were persecuted for having a belief, a religion, a calling, a purpose. Many were shamed, held down, hung, strung up, abandoned, rejected, tormented, and outed in the name of fear and judgment. When all we are here for is LOVE and FORGIVENESS, that's it. Love and forgiveness, pretty simple, huh? It isn't if all you have held onto, lived on, and ran with was FEAR/Fight & flight. Stop holding onto things, perceptions, ideas, and patterns. It's time to let go. It's okay; we have you, we hold you, raise you, and know you. Is this you? This is your soul, ancestors, loved ones, ascended masters, angels, guides and spirits, and GOD. We are all here, we are a team, it's a team effort, and do you want to be part of the light team, team light? Guess what you already are, always have been, and always will be. What is my soul's purpose? Why am I here? What are my passions? What makes me unique? YOU are a child of God. That alone makes you unique, that gives you your soul's purpose, passion, and soul is your DNA.

Find your inner poet, try to channel your soul's voice. They are whispering to you. Our soul is intrinsically tied to our contract with the universe when we enter it. We are the volunteers. Is your inner voice so strong that it screams above the rooftops? You feel an inner burning and desire to share your experiences, your thoughts, your inner knowing's. Sharing your radical light with the world. Guess what? It's not radical! It's who you are. We have been controlled and manipulated to thinking otherwise. Remember when the "me too" movement, when the last gasp of the old order, us collectively standing up, saying me too. It happened to me or a friend or family, acquaintance, etc. When the upper lips don't speak, the lower lips don't either (in reference to being with the wrong partner). How we have been shamed for the loving womb of womanhood, our soul has been stuffed into a box, to be compartmentalized, your soul changed the stars for your legacy and your lifetime. We are the ones who give birth; we came from someone else's body that gave birth to us. To understand the women in our lives, we need to explore this part of who we are. I feel an inherent calling to explore my family lineage, record stories of the Woycenko family (shortened to Woyce by my grandfather to avoid persecution), and then my mom's side of the family. How is it we are slowing down aging wise? We know goddesses never age? Some heavy lifting in the women's department, dress your archetype and your season color (winter/fall, etc.). I'm an anomaly — winter.

54% of the children in the USA have a chronic disease, and their life expectancy is going down! The energy of our soul whispers; it speaks to us all. It radiates outward our inward spirit, our truths, what we are. My soul shrunk as I grew up. I was told I was too much of everything; many who were around me, even raising me, were uncomfortable around me. I brought out their shadows; this makes so much sense now. It was always others and not me. Now I'm not saying I didn't do anything wrong. Those were my feelings, my truth. I own parts of myself that made mistakes, hurt others as I was hurt. I own and take ownership of it all. We need to stop allowing our life force to be released that way, sexual abuse, and more. If our boundaries are leaky, it radiates out to the universe. Please hurt me and abuse me, secrets and shadows. Then we go into abuse of our bodies, our minds, our soul, addictions, and more.

I have had a few mentors in my life, living and not living. Most notably, my Grandmother — Rhoda. I'm just learning that she was highly intuitive as well. She didn't advertise it. Back then, that was taboo or would bring shame/anger as well. So, we have to practice self-love, compassion, openness, and bridging with others to receive all the innate gifts we have. Not against each other but for each other. Where is our value? Do we have to show more skin, gossip, sleaze, shock and awe, reality shows, violence, swearing, backstabbing? I can't even. We can't heal the fast lane until we heal the small stuff — do the inner work. Let's make healing contagious! My feelings of unworthiness kept me stuck in healing in all areas. It's a piece I had to heal many times over, just when I thought I had done so. It's not how many years it took but the journey to get there. Working on mastery, one step at a time, if I didn't go through this, how can I then turn around and teach others to do so as well? I'm a living, breathing experience of being an example and a student of the universe. I shine my light. I'm merely a beacon, a vessel to hold space for others while they heal and walk their healing and spiritual journey. Our soul work is so important, the most important part of our ascension and our intuition. I feel a pull to run away from what, though? I want to roam and be free. As I'm writing this, COVID19 has had its grip on the world since mid-March 2020. As they said, this is the new normal, what is normal. What was happening in the world was not normal. That was ego. It was dark, fearful, running old programs and paradigms that we could not sustain. We are being forced to look within and heal all of those parts of ourselves that we have been running from, distracted from, numbing from. So many restrictions, no international travel, some states are on lockdown, no family gatherings, wearing masks, feeling anxious, feeling alone, I feel disconnected from myself. Maybe disconnected from others as well. I want to help heal the world. Maybe not the world. I'm looking for impact. Is it for notoriety, or is it to truly help and heal?

It's almost July 2020; my son's birthday is July 1st (Canada Day), as I'm Canadian. Yes, Canada Day, all about freedom, patriotism, land of the free, freedom has been coming up too. Freedom, that's really, truly what I crave. I feel compressed in this home shared with my boyfriend; I don't even want to be around him. I'm trying to do so much, and he does nothing. He sits around watching TV or on his phone. It's quite sad that I'm judging him and that I have truly lost respect for him. He is a child, and I attract men who are either hyper-aggressive or lost, if that makes sense? There must be something in me that is unhealed or the need to mother/fix others. There it is, my epiphany, my mirror, in my face, reflecting onto me what I see and feel. Man, I tell you, not cool, not fun, quite depressing at the same time. Feeling like a wild, caged animal, all boxed in, same old bullshit. I'm so tired of this all, doing the same thing, day in and day out. All about my business, nothing about me, when do I get time for myself? When do I get time to explore, to find the softness again, within myself, about myself? Instead of being focused on others, then I feel like I have narcissistic tendencies too. That it's all about me, and I want nothing to do with anyone. I just want to be alone, and I'm tired, I'm worn out, I'm exhausted, even if I haven't worked outside the home since March. I have been busy helping, working, creating, speaking, etc.

Now I'm getting the callback to go back to work, and I don't want to. Just as COVID was hitting, I injured myself at work. It's a very physical job, restocking shelves and rearranging items, so it looks pretty on the shelf, and they make more money. I got golfers elbow, and I wasn't able to do physiotherapy until mid-May. So, it's not 100% healed, and I'm not comfortable going back as I don't want to reinjure my elbow. So, I feel I'm at a crossroads. Now I know why I feel the push to give 100% to my business running in the background, to have at least one new client a week. This will ensure my work and mission continues. It's a deep burning desire, my soul's mission and purpose. I feel so deeply engrained by what I do, what I need to do, what I must do. It's the driving force, my life force, my life's work to keep going. Just as I'm writing this to you, I don't want to go back to the EGO world, the 3D world. I want to help others achieve their beautiful blueprint, their soul's purpose, their life soul print, their natural nature of nurture. You are so divinely held in the eyes and grace of God. There is no right or wrong only discord from what your soul's contract brought you here to do. To push beyond what you think you're capable of doing, that's a box, comfort zone to be extracting the inner sparkles and spark that has always been waiting for you to ever expanse it out into the matrix. The matrix is where all of our gifts lie, our magic incantations that become who we are, who we always have been, and who we immerse ourselves in being.

Let's talk about the inner child, who longs to come out, be heard, valued, seen, and appreciated. To the one that was told to be quiet, to be seen and not heard. Somehow, children had nothing of importance to say, feel, share, and feel valued as a person. I felt that throughout my childhood, so many egos running around dictating that I was too emotional, too sarcastic, too goofy, too silly, too tall, too fat, too smart, too dumb. All these labels and soul oppressions turn into obsessions of thought, habit, and distorted reality. It takes a toll on the psyche and the identity; you start to compartmentalize things into tiny boxes so you can safely and neatly tuck them away. That makes it easier to process than say dealing with the feelings or saying no, that was mean, I won't tolerate that, boundaries my friends, boundaries. Saying NO is a complete sentence. No explanation needed. The wounded inner child, the traumatized inner child, the invalid inner child longs. It craves to be held, to be fawned over, adored, and loved so unconditionally. Otherwise, it turns into addictions, depression, anxiety, panic attacks; it manifests and festers into something else. Like an alter ego, a split, a separation of the mind/body/spirit. For me, it turned into that of a perfectionist, a people pleaser, and an inner critic. The inner critic is not the problem; your inaction is. It stops us from creating things, saying things, and doing things in the world. Discomfort is growth, keeping you from your greatness. Discomfort is birthing pains, and we are all experiencing this. Where did you learn this from, mom, teacher, spouse, and friend?

Maybe your teacher said, oh no, that looks so wrong, or a friend that said, you're not pretty! Internal judgment from the outside, we tend to make assumptions in our minds. The inner critic is no longer part of my persona or inner dialog. You can track where it comes from. Inner critic comes from fear. It stops us first, so we don't get hurt. I'll just stay safe. Why are we scared to move beyond the inner critic? It steers us away from your giftedness in life. Maybe you got labeled the warrior, the pot-stirrer, the one who brought up uncomfortable conversations around the dinner table. The ego knows you won't change, so change the relationship with the inner critic. Ask yourself, what would I gain to move toward myself? What could possibly happen if I surrender to this belief, this block, this trauma? What's the worst thing that could happen?

SOULWORK

Let's try channeling! I know some of us think it's only for us gifted or special folks. That is wrong. We all have the ability to channel sources. It's available to us at any time. All we have to do is ask. So, find a quiet space, meditate for a few minutes, slow your breath down and ask your higher self, ask God, ask your guides, your angels, and your loved ones to come through to assist you. Ask what your soul's purpose is, and wait for it. It will come in lovingly, softly, maybe loudly if you haven't been paying attention to all the signs they have been sending.

You will start to activate your:

Claircognizance (clear knowing).

Clairaudience (clear hearing).

Clairsentient (clear feeling).

Clairvoyance (clear seeing).

Clairalience (clear smelling).

Clairgustance (clear tasting).

Let pen hit the paper and start writing. Keep going, don't think about it. Let me know how it goes. I also have videos on YouTube to assist.

6

INNER CHILD

I have had this struggle for so long, now I'm leading my clients/others through the inner child process (it's July 2020, 3 months into Covid19). Things are very different from pre-covid. I like it, though, and it's given me many realizations and epiphanies. I don't like that people are dying, losing their jobs, families, homes, and perceived way of life. I feel this is a way to rebuild their foundations, start fresh, start new, find out what love is. To come together in a commonplace community, collaboration, and loving each other as they are, not what we think they should be. I'm writing this part in August 2020, and we are five months into COVID19 or, as I like to say, PLANdemic.

I can't believe we are here, at the same time I can. We have been running full-speed ego head for far too long. Now we are at a standstill. Yes, some places have opened up. Some are phasing how businesses open or "back to normal." There is no more normal. We cannot go back.

We are here. There are no more avoiding things, running away, numbing out, addicting out, oh those people trigger me. Why is this happening to me? Victim mode again? I'm done with not having any healing, boundaries, standing in my truth and power. That's where my soul lies in all of that. I'm stepping away from social media too, everyone and everything has an opinion or hair-trigger. I understand we all have a voice, but everyone is shouting above or stepping over people to voice it. This space is too noisy, too much, and does nothing as we are so overwhelmed with all of it. That we don't listen, we don't fully integrate what we're hearing or seeing and forget it all and move on to the next thing we scroll past. That, to me, is keeping us stuck, limited, and not fully appreciating what and who we are at a soul level. We are sparkling shiny souls of which God made us in his eye, his example, his knowing and feeling what true love is. Why don't we love ourselves as God does? Why are we so entrenched in the ego? It started way before our parents started their journey, or our grandparents, great grandparents, etc.

It started multiple, hundreds of past lives ago. That intergenerational trauma started long ago. From what I read from Mark Hyman's book *"It didn't start with you,"* he talks about family trauma and how it was inherited. That we continue to carry and pass it on to the next generation, I like to think, feel that we are stopping it in this generation. Maybe I'm a dreamer, but it starts with me, us, and you. Yes, we can do this. If you're reading this book, you've already started by being curious. Curiosity breeds digging, digging breeds knowing, then acceptance, then release, forgiveness, and healing. That's how we're going to make our way home. By my mentor's words, "Michael Mirdad," three things will set you free "Unconditional Love, Forgiveness, and Healing." That's it, so simple, I know. Somehow our 3D lower vibrational ego-mind trap wants us to think/feel otherwise. That is a lie, that's not true, it's not the unholy trinity's words "religion, science, and politics." I mean, come on, have you ever had a great experience or feeling with any of those? So many of us have been shamed, blamed, damned, cast out, burdened, ridiculed, felt less than, and so on by these "institutions." Yes, they put you in an institutional state of mind, a prison, a fortress of your own doing. Why do that to yourself? Oh, that's right, you have been conditioned, programmed, lied to, kept down, and your freedom is your birthright. Freedom to be who you are, to say what you want, to speak your truth authentically. That's who you are at the core of all of this.

You are so freaking shiny, whole and beautifully made in the core of God's soul. He speaks to you through how you approach or attack yourself. You will be vindicated, walk into the light, be the light, shine the light till it burns and radiates in all the spaces/places that seem heavy or unilluminated (dark). Why cast yourself and others to a place you have already been? Why not try something new, something that is who you truly are, this is your natural state of being, (I keep hearing Billy Joel's song, *"I'm in a New York State of Mind"*) your inheritance. This is your divine birthright. You and God are one, father/mother/holy spirit. That's the holy trinity. That's who you are, who you have always been. Even before birth, you were created in God's image, there lays perfection because of that love, and there is no right or wrong. It just is. Our voice needs to be heard; we are authentic. Being born is our authenticity. It's August 2020 when I'm writing this section, and we are five months into COVID19. We have been upgrading, shedding old programs, releasing fears, intergenerational trauma inherited from family/ancestors, and more. As we shed, we ascend higher and higher. Many of us are waking up, becoming more psychic, intuitive, telepathic, lightworkers, healers that we are all born with. This is who we are at a core level; we are all healing at the same time. I'm learning every day about boundaries and why I never had them. As empathy, we feel people's judgment and disapproval even before we are told. That's just it. We feel, we feel it all. We feel more than you know, or what you think you know, even what you try to hide.

There is no hiding; you are exposed in every way. There is no hiding; we are the lie detectors, the virtual lie detectors. We just don't tell you. There is no point to tell you when you, i.e. because you will deny it. You will hide from it, and you will live in your shame smear campaign until your full exposure breaks it all apart. Apart from what you think you know, from whom you think you are. That right there is a false knowingness based on deception and lies. Our ego smokescreen, just enough to keep you interested, distracted, or hooked to put you in a trance-like mode to stop feeling fully alive to dead. Dead is the ghost in you, that inner smokescreen of the past, living in the past, past of the living dead? Holding onto the ghosts, there is nothing to hold onto. It disappears like vapors, smoke, like thin air. It escapes all reality because you live virtual, working out your next move, your next deception, mainly a deception of self of who you truly are. You are light, you are love, and you are a holy child of God. Yes, you are; the denial, the smokescreen, the façade, the lies, the holding onto the past like it's your soul identification, victimization victimhood, rips the soul apart into little bits of matter. That matter dissipates and gets lost in the smokescreen, the ego system; the ego tries to filter it out. It merely gets caught in the energy swirls of your being. It swirls round and round, and it's always there waiting to be magnetized, expanded, and constructed back into your particulate self. Your soulful, soul-fed self, that magical bits of you are interwoven back into who you are at a soul level. You are the truth, the light, the love of God. God is that in you. It has always been this way. Why do you run? What do you fear?

Fear is ghost vapors of what was, what was fed, trained, engrained, and false. This is not who you are. Child of God, do you hear me? I'm calling, whispers and whimpers not fully readied and steadied by the ear. Its minuet — it's fleeting, just like our virtual life, this is by design, but designed by who? Ah, now we're digging deeper, uncovering what was, what is, now and fully present to be seen by the eyes of a child. That's where we start. We are born again, resurrected, no longer crucified by man. Man has no idea what this means. That's too OUT there; therefore, you're out there and cannot be in here. You're crazy. Yes, crazy for following the illusion for far too long, the herd, and going with the flow did not mean undermining every core belief and value you have. That was imprinted into you by God. That imprint was forcibly untraceable, and they tried to unwrite it. It is ingrained into every fiber of your being, your strands of golden elixir poured into by God almighty, the Holy Spirit, father-mother God. This cannot be undone. Except you undo it. Ego identity, being programmed, your ancestors, parents, family, friends, school, work colleagues, society, government, religion, and science. It is all exposed now, and there is no going back. We are unraveling at a hyper speed, unraveling into unknown depths of perception and self. Where this will go, I have no idea. Yes, that's the truth. Isn't that why you're reading this?

Go back to your fairy tales, for that is a smokescreen. Yes, it's all romantic, beautiful, and misleading. That's what they want, you to be misled and off of the truth of who you are, why you're here, and it's your mission, your duty, your calling, your team/the collective is calling your name. Do you not hear it, dear one? We are here, waiting for you to turn the light on, go green, let's go, and the lights are on, all aboard. This cruise is not in control. It's cruising at a soul speed. What is the speed, only by which the depths of your healing, forgiving, relationship healings at all levels, all levels, you will feel lighter, brighter, like the weight of the world is off your shoulders? It never was; that's your twisted, deluded, programmed thinking. Time to rewire and live inspired. That inspiration is your divinity, your birthright, your magic, your truth, your freedom, and your sovereignty to get there. Where is there exactly? It is by no means wrong or right, up or down, do this, take that. It's highly individualized and at a collective conscious level. Merging one into light with others, raising the global resonance of love, love is highly regarded as the only thing that will cure what ails us all. Yes, ails us. We suffered a global sickness. We are here for a reason. I told you this. It took me my lifetimes and hundreds of lifetimes to figure this out. Not that I know all and have the secret, there are no secrets, only love unrecognized. I'm training to be a Chaplain now. Fast forward to 2020. Covid19 hit March 11, 2020. Life as we know it will never be the same again. Why should we go back to normal? I don't want to go back to normal.

Normal is why we're here! We don't love unconditionally. We don't trust, forgiveness for self and others, and to heal! There is no separation, we are not separate, and we forgot who we were at a soul level, unlimited spiritual beings having a human experience. We have to become accountable and responsible. If I continually do the things that my ancestors taught me, spirit shows up and says, uh, no, you can do better! Trust your intuition, listen to those little nudges, God throws pebbles, then he throws bricks. Are you living your life as the truth of who you are? We need to be responsible! *There are four essentials of trust: trust in self, trust in God, trust in others, and trust in life.* Vulnerability is the core of trust. The first thing I need to know is that I'm a unique demonstration and representation of the chief architect and creator of the universe. All God is what I am. Otherwise, I will continue to believe in separation, that we are separate and we have separated. The gift of 2020 is that I see God again, felt God again, and know God is, I AM, we are. That is what 2020 taught me. Oh, yes, I was a medium, psychic, healer, coach, mentor, and more. At the core, I AM, so are you, so are we. We are all connected at a core level; I heard the call to serve others, to be in service for others. "How may I serve?" I asked, and God showed me. I need to grow and expand in my practice through prayer, prayer for others, prayers for myself, prayers to God. I was being guided to level up, ascend the tree of life, stay focused, stay in trust, stay in peace, don't look down, look up, keep climbing, don't extend out to the branches, stay on the trunk, the trunk is strong.

The anchor against the wind, the rain, the fires, the dust — the roots of our past, our presence in our future fully focused on the truth of who we are. (Internal compass is the voice of God.) We have to learn to trust others. Others are a representation of God. Human beings are messy as heck, but they teach us, each other, mirrors and reflections, give us an opportunity to grow something they need is something they learn. Trusting who God is as our childhood, especially if God's image was taught to us, as vengeful and kept us in scarcity, fear, control, and direct conflict with our internal compass. The further off our compass, the darker the road. Be willing to piss people off, sound different, look different, be unique and shake people's foundations and judgments to the core. Understand God's nature. When you're ready to step into a new place, that you're so scared that you pee yourself. *That's when you will depend on something greater than you. If you don't have pee running down your leg, and then you're NOT living BIG, authentically. Iyanla Vanzant* Keep on walking, keep trusting, and keep having faith. When you know you lie, then you don't trust. Trust in yourself. Trust in God that you will always land on your feet. Rebuilding ourselves starts with stripping down our foundation. Maybe it blew up; maybe it was stripped down slowly. The great news is, you can start over again, you can reclaim, and it will claim you. Our old foundations were built on weak premises, old trauma, wounds, ancestral stuff, and ego glass all around. Start with a solid, stable ground built with love, and the beautiful colorful mosaic will gather.

Family doesn't get special dispositions just because they are blood. Don't keep trusting or betray yourself just because they are related to you. Boundaries, I'm sure your family betrayed you on some level, whether it's in this lifetime or past lives. I'm the one who made it out; everyone has their hands out when they see you rising. Through demonstration in relationships, if you are involved with someone who cannot keep their word or complete what they started. You may want them to be there for you. You can see that they can't, they don't have the capacity to live at the level I'm living, it's not like they are a bad person, and they are a different level of understanding than you are. It's not love to ask someone to do something they are unwilling or unable to do. It's love to see them for who they are and release any expectations. Superiority & Inferiority plus dishonesty is the root of all racism. Trace this back to our ancestors, our roots. We bypassed the racism issue to unconditional love & forgiveness. We didn't deal with it head-on. We need to have honest conversations. I feel the presence of God when I breathe. I experience love when I'm present. The purpose of forgiveness is to elevate my consciousness. I'm living my purpose when I put God first. My life force is most fulfilled when I'm praying. I love to pray. It's a beautiful space that's not in the physical. I'm not a woman, I'm not poor, I AM one with God. The biggest obstacle to peace is JUDGMENT.

The most difficult choice I've had to make to fulfill my destiny is to say no to my family patterns. ONE word to describe who you are and why you're here is "trust" The reason we need to trust is, it keeps us connected to God. Just like the baby bird leaping from its nest, the baby bird trusts and knows instinctively its time. It's a lesson to trust our wings, and we too will soar. This I know to be true, like Bette Midler once sang, *"You are the wind beneath my wings"* Fly...fly...fly away.

SOULWORK

What was your first trauma? Do you remember? Did you subconsciously block it out?

Do you have nightmares? Were you teased or bullied (what did they say or do?)?

What is keeping you from your magic? Do you know?

Any of these feelings? Judgment, worry, overwhelm, negativity, status, anger, money, anxiety, blame, shame, unworthy, busyness, avoidance, and numbing.

Replace Judgement with Freedom, Worry with Trust, Negativity with Positivity, Status with Grounded, Lack with Abundance, Blame with Innocence, Shame with Glory, Unworthiness with Honor (worthy), Guilt with Innocence, Avoid with Allow, Numbing with Intuitive, Busyness with Available, Fight with surrender, Flight with Standing, Scared with Brave, Anger with Peace, and Grief with Bliss

7

FINDING MY WINGS

Funny about the title of this chapter, I can hear my guides say you always had them. Your wings were always there, hidden, buried underneath all that stuff. The weights of inner turmoil, of others' thoughts, opinions, judgments, and expectations. *"Don't worry about what people think of you. When you come to the end of this life, you're not going to stand before people. You're going to stand before God!"* How it all enmeshed into who I thought I should be, who I never felt I was like I'm in the wrong body, the wrong mind sometimes. I feel the trappings of a madwoman, fighting to be heard, to be seen, by whom I ask? By my soul, my soul has always been here.

I just wasn't listening or paying attention, distracted, dismissive, medicated, numbed out on alcohol or some junk food, some social media post, some escapism TV post, oh, look at me, and look at what I'm doing. I'm so amazing, yes, that's me, why do I need or want all the attention? Why does this trigger me? This comes from my parental inattention. They had their own shit to deal with and sort out. They tried their best, and I do not blame them. I feel I blame myself for not seeing this sooner or faster, get a grip, see here comes my inner critic, so quick to judge, so quick to be harsh, so quick to hold my feet on the fire and say, "SEE you fucked up again? I knew it, couldn't be trusted to help yourself, couldn't trust yourself, READY…FIRE, where's the AIM?" As I prepare to move yet again, I'm going through all of my stuff and realize all the shit I hold onto holds me down. Why do I keep it, for sentimental reasons, a memory or longing to hold onto something that made me feel good for a minute? I'm looking to feel good every day, every minute, to be blissfully joyful because I AM. That alone is just perfect enough for me to share that with others and help them radiate it inward, up, and out-ward.

It's Mid October 2020 when I write this, and we had our first snowfall of the season. Need to get out of here quick, or do I stay, wait five months until winter is done? A lot of things will be done. Why wait on someone else? He doesn't wait for me. He carries on like I'm not here, the occasional poke when "I'm Grumpy." So immature.

I no longer desire to have any relationships with anyone that does not lift me. So how do I find my wings? By clipping away all the debris, the negativity, the insecurities of myself and others, think of it as dead weight. As I heal, grow, and expand, I feel lighter, I feel brighter, and I feel like my encapsulated self, an embodiment of a crystalline body. I no longer hold a carbon 3D body, and I cannot sustain this heaviness, this weight of the world. I speak about my broken identity, identities, and guess what? You are loved and cherished. We somehow fragmented our consciousness, seen ourselves separate from source, from God, from who we are. Know that you are cherished, and everything else is, is a lie. The one law of love permeates my being. Slice away anything that is not the truth, the karmic patterns, and the intergenerational trauma. To be born again, coming into the spirit so that every day when you wake up, erase everything from your mindset. No, not today. I'm a new being, new spirit, and new love to the most high God. Watch your life change right before your eyes, this love frequency. Get rebirthed into the spirit. I never realized this TRUTH until now, spoken to me through a zoom meeting, the whisperings of myself, climbing back to who I AM. The truth of it all, the truth of God, I AM as God created me, and I will be the Christ on earth. This is truly who I was reborn to be, not born, born, rebirthed — new.

This is me, all shiny again, like a baby; I'm born, reborn, and a cherished child. I AM the embodiment of crystalline light, light codes, light body, lightening the load to reintegrate new frequencies. Now I feel like I'm channeling, channeling my soulful self. This is who I AM. Channeling for all, for all to hear, as you can channel too. I feel like I'm going home, I want to go home, I'm already home? Is this true? Of course, it is. Why wouldn't it be? This is a time of pause, reflection, going through desert places in between climbing the mountain. There is always a force sustaining us, always moving us forward. God gives us grass through the desert. Without God breathing in his direction, he didn't stop the trouble, but he kept the trouble from stopping me. We can get overwhelmed; God comes in with a person to lighten the load. That's why this pandemic has not stressed you out, kept you down, or separated you. While you're waiting, God's making the hard places easier. Without his favor, your trouble would overwhelm you. No matter what you go through, divorce, betrayal, sickness, job loss — God is our rock, our favor, our savior, and always sustaining us. I just learned from a friend that "Kristos" is a Greek name for Boys, is a variant form of Christopher (Greek) follower of Christ — Anointed One — bearing Christ. And Christine is part of the Kristos variant. I love all of this, finding origins and connections to one's name. It feels so personal, refreshing, about to get a second wind. How do I make it through any difficult time? Time to step into a green pasture God has already prepared. The time is now, this is your time, like the Phoenix rising from the ashes, and you are reborn again and again. You have learned from your past, your ancestors.

This is your time to rise and shine. Time to transmute all of the pain, all of the fear, all of the anger, all of the injustice, all of it is being cleared now. Please know we are here to lift you, think of me, think of God, think of the collective. We are all connected through collective thought, telepathy, and prayer. We cannot sustain any more negativity. Lord, thank you for the green pastures, thank you for coming through, and for sustaining me when I should have gone under. Thank you for defeating much bigger enemies. Thank you for giving me the stamina to outlast the opposition. It looks like I'm channeling the utmost high, God, Christ, and the Holy Spirit with a side of St Germain, Archangel Michael, Mother

Mary, and Mary Magdalene. In those desert places, you don't know what God has for you. Don't believe ego lies; it wants to keep you stuck, keep you dark, and keep you down. You have the power to outlast and try, try, try again. God made the green pastures for you to lie in. Your future is brighter than the past; this is all a part of your destiny. Without his desert, you cannot fulfill your destiny, the fullness of your destiny! I'm not settling for mediocrity, suffering, negativity, or feeling stuck. I decree and declare you are flourishing in God's favor. Wow, it's November 2020 already, and my tricky ego says, how long will it take you to write this book? Why is it taking so long? So many other people have their book out or have written ten books. Look at you, starting a million things and not finishing them. Procrastinator, fraud, etc.

Anyways, that's my dialog sometimes, one minute, I'm on top of the world and amazing, and the other, nope, nada, no good. So, I'm siding on the optimist, the love, the learning to roll with it, flow with it and go for it. The older our thoughts are, the more they have weight and punch you in the gut sort of speak. This old thought, trauma, is deeply rooted, deep within, looping feedback into our minds and keeping us attached to guilt. It's a hidden attraction. We try to compare ourselves to others, keeping us in victim mentality. We have left 2020; we are now entering 2021 as I'm writing this. I keep saying I'm writing a book, and yet I kept procrastination, unworthiness, inner critic, and imposter syndrome drive the ship. I accept this as old programming, labels, and energy I'm committed to doing. 2020 at the beginning of a new year, instead of resolutions, to break. I decided on a word, a feeling, and used that word to be the center, the focal point of a vision board, a dream board, a blueprint, a map, a key to my soul's purpose. My word for 2021 and my feeling is Intention. The intention is a feeling attached to an idea and then going forward. A thing or a plan, a thing intended and the healing process of a wound. That was a powerful connection for me as 2020's word was Rebirth. It truly was and is.

I intend to keep writing, documenting my series, and navigating through 2021, like 2020 wasn't enough? I just finished hosting a live show all about near-death experiences. I'm so fascinated by it. And now have several speakers on the topic, a hospice nurse, a death doula, and it's amazing. Death is never final; it's the destination point but not the end, just the beginning.

SOULWORK

I highly recommend writing a letter to your inner child. Start with a meditation on your own, a quiet space, maybe in nature, or part of an inner sanctuary you have. (I have this meditation on my Sound cloud account and YouTube @24khealing)

It is best to have a notepad, journal, piece of paper to write on. You may keep this letter, write multiple letters, or burn it. You may reference the outline that I use and go back whenever something comes up.

DEAR SWEET CHILD, I WANT YOU TO KNOW…

How much I love you, unconditionally and always.

What keeps you up at night as a child? What keeps you up now?

What were your fears as a child? Were they yours? Was it your mom, your dad, siblings, teachers, friends, or other families?

What was magical to you as a child? What is now?

What did you dream of as a child, being, and imagining, playing, doing? Who was your first friend (real or imaginary or both)?

Which elementals were you drawn to? (Unicorns/Gnomes (earth), Fairies, fireflies (air), Dragons (fire), Mermaids (water)

What was your first memory as a child? How old were you?

Did you feel loved unconditionally, safe, and accepted?

Let go, visualize, relax, and meditate.

POEM "CALL TO THE INNER CHILD"

Dear Beautiful child of past-present and future. This I know to be true, I love you. You're my first and true love. I take you with me as I go about my day. Learning to be curious and play. I'm getting my head out of the way. Unraveling what I think I know to knowing, I trace back the steps of wonderment and enchantment from doing to BEING. Forever looking through my eyes, back into yours, relishing all the goodness that has always been. I feel love, kindness, compassion, faith, and joy. I'm permeating in exuberance, empathy, play, zest, and patience. Fairies, dragons, Unicorns, and Mermaids into my swirling imagination; leaves tiny imprints forever merging to my Soul's remembrance.

Now write a letter to your inner child with your non-dominant hand. Why? Because it will look like a child wrote it, that has an impact.

My clients' work has shown something that was buried, forgotten, or wiped from memory. Only to resurface, be seen, be heard, be felt, and be healed.

8

CODEPENDENCY

On Dec 1, 2020, I left a six-year relationship. I sold 90% of what I had and packed up my car, and drove 1200 miles west. Heading west to my birthplace, where my grandparents built their beautiful home back in the 1960s. Oh, did I mention I brought my 22-year-old son with me! The first two months were magical, almost like I was in a dream state or dreaming. Then reality crashes down into regret, panic, anxiety. Did I make a mistake? Staying true to myself, boundaries, and co-dependency is a thing for me. The greatest addiction is codependency, and boy did I suffer from it. Why? Due to no boundaries!

Not everyone has an addiction to food, alcohol, medication, sex, etc. Notice the similarity to spiritual teachings around the world. Human beings believe they are separate from God and others, this creates a sense of emptiness, and that emptiness has to be dealt with in some way. Either anxiousness or depression, we feel off.

We need to feel sedated or stimulated. Either way, we feel empty, no matter how many times we try to fill up. I was trying to fill up the emptiness with addiction, something outside of me. I'm dependent on something, people dependant, I have forgotten who I am, I feel empty inside, anything, anyone, anything outside of me make me feel different. We all become reactive and neurotic, hyper anxious and trying to fix everything. Everything outside is what makes us feel off, and responsibility takes it the other way. Like religion is missing something, they don't know how to create the solution, fill with the presence of God, and then I'm filled with myself, I'm here, I'm awake. We wake up and show up! Only three relationships — God – self – others (that's it).

Sufi says the connection with spirit comes first, then self, then others — those three, working on all three at one degree or another. When we feel empty, it's a karmic loop; we blame others or something outside of me. I have come to learn that co-dependency is addiction, in fact, the #1 addiction. Why do I say this? For me, I was always looking outside of myself for answers, for people to help me, things to help me, food, alcohol, sex, and money to help me alleviate what and how I was feeling. All the trauma I stored and tucked away in neat little boxes, never to be opened again. Or so I thought, with all the things I tried to hide away, would bubble up, resurface, and many times blow up in my face. I then would be traumatized all over again. Life is trauma, the trauma of what was, what is, what should be, how I would have rose-colored glasses only to have them ripped off again, smashed to bits. I have come to realize with all my work with clients and on myself is that many times our anger toward others is anger toward ourselves. The beating of the soul, why did you do that, why didn't you do this, oh look at you — you messed up again. Why don't you know your worth? Quit giving yourself to everyone and everything, like hey look at me, please pick me, because I didn't pick or choose myself. Good God! Why didn't he love me the way I loved him? Why didn't he fight for me the way I fight for him? Why? When we fully see that it's ourselves, we're angry at, frustrated, and want to scream, yell, cry, throw, and smash things to pieces. To do the proverbial zero-point earth, the big bang, to restart the whole universe. Zero-point love, love is the point, and that is what we are guided by. Love only, sweet enveloping love of the purest forms. To be as God created you, to know that and remember that at the beginning of your soul's contract and meandering to the next point, the next path, the next sign, the next fork in the cosmic road.

This soul is racing toward zero point. Zero-point is no end, no beginning; all love, purity, clarity, peace, and presence rolled into my soul makeup. Setting boundaries is the best cure for co-dependency. We don't seem to realize the most rampant disease on the earth is co-dependence. It is the greatest addiction; may I say the number one addiction. Even though all addictions have the same genesis, co-dependence is the easiest to access. I feel it has the same definition as all the other addictions, which is this. And notice the similarity of spiritual teachings throughout the world from various teachers. Notice how they all connect. Human beings believe that they are separate from God and each other. And this creates a sense of emptiness inside. That emptiness is going to need to be dealt with in some way.

Our emptiness becomes either anxiousness or depression. We feel this emptiness. We feel off. We feel something, and then we start to feel anxious or depressed. Then we feel the need to fill the holes of our soul with outer things. We didn't realize we had energy leaks leaking here and there that no number of addictions will ever fill. If we feel anxious, we're going to need to be sedated. If we start to feel depressed, we need to feel stimulated. So, everybody's looking for some form of that. Numbing out or up.

The problem is, we feel empty. We reach out for something to fill the emptiness. Nothing fills the emptiness, so we go and try it again. That's addiction. As soon as you try to fix something using a synthetic, not just synthetic chemically, synthetic meaning outside of ourselves, you're in a cycle. You're in a pattern, and it's endless because one needs to feed the other.

As soon as I feel empty and I try something, and it doesn't fill me. Oh, my God, I'm desperate! I'm even emptier and more desperate. I need it. I need even more of it. And there you go, off into addictions, instead of feeling the feeling of emptiness, letting it go and replace it with the fullness of love, the refilling of your cup. Empty it, and then refill it. But not all of us choose drugs or alcohol or food or whatever. We do not realize that our relationships are riddled with and rampant, filled with this same problem, this emptiness.

And what it's called is co-dependence. Co-dependence means I have become dependent — I'm drug-dependent — I'm alcohol-dependent — I'm food-dependent — I'm people-dependent. And more people are people dependent than any other addiction. I want to stuff away all my feelings into all these addictions to not truly look at the soul, to dig deep into the vastness of who I am. What does it mean to be people dependent? It means, "I have forgotten who I am. I feel an emptiness inside, and I really would appreciate it if you, anyone, anything outside of me could make me feel better. I feel down; pick me up. I feel up; take me down a bit. It's such a see-saw of emotions that make you feel sick inside. The swirling merry go round of co-dependence.

Or, as relationships go, you make me feel so wonderful. Or you are the blame for me not feeling wonderful." See, that's all co-dependent because it's not interdependent. It's not responsible. It's reactive to things on the outside. So we have been hardwired, stimulated, and brainwashed to reactivity. That's the go trap. Oh, I have to respond to every nuance, every thought, every feeling and distract it, reflect it, deflect it.

So, feel it that way. Co-dependence is like that. We feel we're empty, and then we start reacting to and becoming dependent upon people. If people don't like us, it's depressing. If people are upset with us, that's anxiety-creating. We become very reactive and neurotic. The reaction is a response system. We have to fill this void somehow. We become hyper-anxious and trying to fix everything. Because if it's off, we're off. The problem is, we keep thinking everyone outside, or everything outside is what's making us feel off. Responsibility takes it to the source. So maybe we're feeling off. We're feeling disconnected from each other, from love, from God. We're feeling disconnected from answers, solutions, and healings. Truly disconnected from our perfect wholeness, that's what God created, so therefore you are. Like looking for our next hit, where can we get this? In a way, we need science or religion, reason it away, as it's almost a form of a spiritual or mental aspirin to deal with pain. Of course, they scoff and say it's all a joke. It's all false, and they think there's nothing to it. They are thinking, rather feeling and knowing and trusting it's already there. They are missing something too.

They're missing God, and the religions are missing God all too often even though they talk about God like it's something outside of them or in the sky and out of reach, somewhat unattainable, like a mirage in the desert. Often, they don't know how to create the solution, to see, know, and feel the vision, which is to be filled with the presence of God.

And as I'm filled with the presence of God, I start to be filled with the presence of me, myself. I'm here. I'm awake, and anything that happens, I'm aware that it's my doing. It's a reflection of my experience inside, and that's when we start to wake up and show up again. We become responsible. So, I guess I'm taking responsibility for how I feel, how I behave, and how I see myself. Through God's eyes, there is only love. So, therefore, I'm love too.

SOULWORK

Boundaries are necessary, are love and are a vibration you put out. Like a homing signal, either saying I'm not worthy, take advantage of me OR I know who I'am, why I'm here and I'm so worth it! They do not push people away, they are love, they are not selfish, they are not mean, they don't take up a lot of time and people won't like you less.

Think of anything or anyone you are co-dependant (definition: dependence on the needs of or control by another) Jot it down, reminisce, reflect and become curious, ask why? No shaming or blaming, we are no longer victims, we are responsible and accountable. Forgive yourself and remember what that feels like, that's how we rework our guts, spidey senses, our intuition! Do you have a hard time saying no? Do you feel guilty or shamed? Do you say yes, when you want to say no? Do you feel yucky when saying no? All of these are signals; you are out of alignment with self.

Practice in the mirror, saying no. Make a song out of it, write a poem or short story. Watch how people respond when you say no, do they respect it? Do they ask repeatedly or do they dismiss you and get angry? These are all tell-tale signs. How did you do?

Feel free to share with me at Christine.gold

9

MAKING MY WAY HOME

I see a building in my dreams. I had never seen it before; somehow, I felt I had been. I was floating above it, all around it, and taking it all in. It was another lifetime, past life long ago. Who knows, I asked my spirit team to assist me in finding out where this place was. One day it appeared on Google in a news story about the history of this building in historic Kaslo, British Columbia, Canada. This iconic hotel hidden in the Kootenay Mountains was so majestic looking, with a bit of haunting charm and a lot of history. So, I decided I was going to visit. I did.

In August 2020, I went. It was amazing to see it in person, a soul remembering. A time to pause and reflect and know that I have been here before, and I felt at home, like shifting westward was the goal and inner vision in mind to begin with. I just had to find the time to slow the fuck down, shut the fuck up, and get my ego bullshit out of the way. Truly, that's a gift, people. An after the anger, rage, resentment toward ourselves for playing small and acting less than. We decide to shift into a new perspective, an inner vision of who we already are. After all the crying, wailing, and forgiveness of self and that breaks the chains. Forgiveness for others, which stops the poison injected upon others, hoping it would inflict death, pain, or suffering on the unforgiven, actually causes a boomerang effect back to you. All the broken relationships that started on false pretenses that I knew were damaged just as much as I was. We were hoping that our co-dependencies would heal ourselves, somehow. Today my office is by the sea, and this is my final resting place. It sounds kind of morbid, really a death. Death is transformation. We are creating a new shiny soulful diamond crystalline self buried in the trappings of the ego life. This is buried in deep darkness only to be revealed in the light. What is constant suburbia of euphoria? What is euphoria? It's when you're dancing and singing like no one's watching, feeling the flow of life and flowers of beauty. Jesus is love, love is me, and you are love. As the sea breeze blows, I'm reminded of how close I am to nature.

Now I know why I never wanted to go home after visiting my grandparents. It was a magical place. It was a safe place, a safe space to expand and explore who this light body named Christine is. I long for the sea, and the sea is the vitamin of my soul. Now I have my 22-year-old son with me, and he, too, is searching for his space. I hope he finds it; he is leagues ahead of where I was. Of course, all mothers think that, smarter, taller, wiser, etc. I truly believe he is a shaman; he just needs to know it. That comes with experience, I want him to experience this for himself, and all I can do is lead by example. He is getting it. He sees and tells me he sees me healing and expanding. That makes him want to do the same, like moths to a flame. That is the feeling I'm going for. To inspire me will therefore inspire others. To be a shining light and example for others to know, see and feel. To know deep down inside there is always hope, that hope leads to faith, faith leads to source. Source is all I want to feel in my life, knowing this is my truth, honor, sovereignty, and sanctuary. Being aware of when I'm not living from my authentic self, soul, heart, and love that has always been here, waiting for you like the faithful doggy waiting for little Susie to come home from school. That's the kind of excitement, awe, and wonder I'm connecting with. The inner child is unleashed, loved, honored, recognized, mattered and cared for, and seen always. To live each day like it's our last best day ever. The toes are splaying out on the sand with each step I take in the sand, on the beach, amongst the waves, getting a natural pedicure, the only way to go, truly!

You must experience the sea before you pass onto another lifetime, reincarnation or right to God. God is waiting with open arms always. He does not wish what the ego wishes — Death, Destruction, and Disease (the Triple D effect). He wishes only the love, the peace, the joy, the bliss, the abundance, the faith, the zero point, the Zen moment. That moment where time stops and nothing is outside of your peripheral vision, seeing everything in a kaleidoscope of colors and wonderment and enchantment, waves and ripples of pure color bliss. The aura effect, your link to your energy and soul — your boundaries are found there. To experience healed energy self is to be fully realized. That is such a pivotal moment to see.

The moment is yours to be fully seen at any time. We must learn to let go of what we thought we were to become, to align with what the collective had already envisioned us to be. They are just waiting on the sidelines, cheering you on! The universe always had your back. You just didn't feel it. Now you do. It's a full transference of the energy of what you are, fully into being the now moment, from moment to moment. Can you feel that? Do you know that? Do you hear that? Do you smell that? Do you taste that? If not now, dear child, then when, all systems light up that inner Christmas tree. Ready, set, go!

SOULWORK

"Prayer takes the ordinary to the extraordinary."
Caroline Myss

For me, Prayer has been my silent, sacred walk with the divine. Each time I pray, I'm learning to become the miracle God had instilled in me. It creates a holy instant, instant connection to all things holy. Prayer does not beg, grovel or barter. Rather it asks us to set up a space within, an inner sanctuary to access through.

Clutter will keep you from your "inner sanctuary."

Do you have spaces or places in your home and life that need a refresh, a detox, a clearing out? Start looking around, especially the bedroom. The bedroom should be a sanctuary, a peaceful place, and a spot to rest. If you keep it cluttered, too warm, too cold, full of electronics or other means of stimulation. How can you relax?

Do a room-by-room detox. Start with your bedroom. Look at ways to green it up, light it up or mellow it out. Feng Shui will give you great ideas and inspirations as well. Let me know how it goes via my Facebook page. https://www.facebook.com/24khealing

10
NEW BEGINNINGS

I feel I have come out the other side to transmute all the pain I have seen, contracted for, felt and now I'm letting go, as they say, letting God. It wasn't an easy transition, and truly I wouldn't have learned a damn thing if I hit the fast forward switch. Really what's the fun of arriving at said destination when the meandering journey is deeper? It's the deep soul dive into the great unknown abysses of being, of knowing, of feeling that we are all connected so very deeply to each other, like the roots of a tree. There is no ending or beginning. Where does it start, where does it end, where does it begin? There is no answer. Only you know, along with God, your collective team of guides/angels/loved ones and ancestors.

I'm enjoying listening to a local Washington radio show KSQM 91.5, it reminds me of the times I spent with my grandmother and mother listening to the "oldies" the classics, and truly I know this is the real music of our lives. I just finished listening to Jerry and the Pace-makers, then John Denver, very eclectic, I know. I have been writing this book for three years now, and it's a life-long remembering of a soul contract. I always feel an excess nagging in my mind, write your book, and write your book. I was reminded by a guest on my podcast, *The Power of Healing Your Energy.* He is a well-known medium, Shawn Leonard. He said, "the spirit is watching; finish your book." I tell ya, the spirit is always watching, guiding, supporting, and cheering you on! It's almost an ego. I catch myself knowing this is something I must do. As part of me not hiding anymore, to put words out for someone else to read them. To extend a gift of freedom through reading this book about the dark night, there is a soul remembrance, a remembering, waking up and saying, hey, what the heck happened here? Why was I asleep for so long? Or was I asleep for so long? What a dream? We are now making our dreams come into the illusionary reality, the reality that we decided to choose our soul, to choose to live, truly living.

Living in God's light, walking in the truth of who God is, of who I AM, who we are. I have come to know this in my new beginning; everything somehow seems brighter, lighter, like a collective weight, not carrying the world on my shoulders. It's not mine to carry. I have my baggage. When I deal with that, then I'm able to help someone else with theirs, and so on. That's how my new beginning looks like, that my worth is not tied to anything or anyone. That's freedom through non-attachment practice. What I mean is not swinging in or out of attached and detached, finding the zero Buddha point. Boy, the world tries to trigger me or find those buttons to push; I choose to see them momentarily and then not. It's like resist not evil, explained eloquently by one of my mentor's Michael Mirdad, *to not be fighting evil and not be scared of evil either*. Like shadow hunting/stalking/running — to see it and fully see it and know what it is and then turn away, not ignoring per se but not giving it credence or acknowledgment. Then there's the other when it blatantly tries to chase you, hurt or scare you — you turn around and say STOP or NO. That alone is standing in your sovereignty, wielding your armor of God, the breastplate of love, the sword of truth, the shield of protection, the sandals of stability, and the helmet of divinity. Wow, just saying that image. Can you see it, own it, and know it? I know I can. I put that on every day and walk in the truth of who I am. And the truth of who you are, Oh holy child of beautiful perfection and love. This beginning looks scary at first because the comfort of the past of staying safe is comforting. Or is it? It reminds me of the pacifier for the child. If it's kept too long, it starts to cause damage to the teeth.

Just like staying comfortable in our discomfort or in our little boxes that keep people out and be safe. God whispers and says, step out, beautiful child of God. You are safe wherever you go; I'm with you always. For you are me, and I am you. The light burns so brightly; it's hard for people to see. They see something, and some look away, frightened it might hurt them. Others are mesmerized by it, and they cannot look away. Either way, I have changed; I'm shiny; I'm new — the person I was at the beginning. It's how one describes a near-death experience; you cannot put it into words. It is your experience, and it cannot be experienced by anyone else. That never left me. It's a soul wake-up call, shake up, let's go. What the heck, I'm gobsmacked by the pure realized soul that I AM! I have much work to do, and I will be run off my feet in pure joy and ecstasy of all the things I will do, through God, through me. I know this is what I'm supposed to be doing, to be sharing, to know at a soul level. This is my calling. What's my human story? It is evolving. I'm answering a very specific call to fully step into who I am authentically. I have a burning desire, and I think about my spiritual journey all the time. So yes, I speak to spirit all the time, sometimes I don't listen. We all need to find the space, the spaces in between, and the spaciousness; there, we find spirit messages. I'm aligning with the highest possible vibration; I'm getting to the core of my reality.

The in-between world, apathy, and compliancy, really feel it out. I'm understanding, innerstanding, and entertaining all sorts of awareness. Be aware of any resistance to anything or anyone. What are the things you are resistant to right now? People, feelings, trauma, smoking, in-laws, food, alcohol, job, etc. Resistance is anything we over-analyze, confusable, or ruminating over and over. I know I have some; now I'm really digging in. Ready to live life fully, raw, expanded, joyfully, blissfully, childlike wonderment. Why? Because we have one life, yes, some of us have had multiple lifetimes. What I'm saying is, isn't it time to feel the butterflies again. Be the not knowing but brave enough to step in and realize who you are? Fully show up, unapologetically, feel the spring in your step for no reason outside of yourself other than the radiant beauty you are, the soul infusion of unconditional love, forgiveness, and healing all parts of you to helpfully help someone else. Guide the way, light the way, bring light, be the light, always, radically way showing. Quantum Jedi master, slay those demons, get behind me, Satan and not today. This should be your everyday mantra! Your form-fitted tagline for your heart's desire. This is where your magical wonderful you shows up and says, "let's play," and the child giggles excitedly back, saying, "yes, you have come home, you're ready to play again, you found me, I found you." It's wonderful to know you again, see you again, and fully live in the wonderment again. Meandering in all the mud pies, drinking from the water hose, riding bikes into the night, swinging the swings, and twirling till you fall.

Laying in the grass looking up into the sky, watching the clouds float by, seeing the dragons, the fairies, and the faces within the clouds. That is a connection back to source because you are fully present in the now moment, moment, by moment created by you and co-created with the universe. You are the magician, and the mind is thy wand. Wield it now and step into your magic, wonder child. I have come home to align, trust, surrender, and awaken to the truth of God. God is within me, always has been. I needed those traumatic experiences for me to have those layers, those pieces ripped apart or blown apart, to fully reveal my nature. I was reminded today by the spirit that my purpose is in the words that I write, speak, and share. This channeled memoir is my authentic self-exposing and showing up for others to find their voice and claim it. Getting myself out of the way because it's not about me, to stop overthinking everything, or having an attachment to how it should be written. I have life; therefore, I have purpose. I don't need a label, accreditation, certification, accolade, or praise for me to know this as the truth of who I AM. I spin and interweave each moment to moment, word by word, feeling by feeling, into the now moment. I truly just exposed myself now. In our family, I felt I had to do better than everyone else because I never felt the approval of my parents or my peers. Man, I wore that like a giant shiny button or badge that said, take advantage of me, abuse me, because I'm the victim.

Boy, those rose-colored glasses are tossed out, putting my reframes on. Reframing every aspect of who I was supposed to be, who I thought I would be, who I pretended to be, faking it to make it, for whom? Was it worth it? Absolutely not! Except for seeing the bullshit narrative on paper right now, oh, I could bypass it or dissect it and beat myself up. No, I now take a compassionate look at myself and say I did the best I could with what I had. Now I have so much knowledge, experience, and lessons to fill up the spaces that feel off, bravely go there and shine a light on it and say, hey, that's new, let's explore. Instead of slamming the door, running away, or denying it's even happening, or maybe it will go away, but it doesn't. I'm not looking for anything or anyone to "fix" anything because it's perfectly imperfect. It's on me to look into and see if this is mine, or is this someone else's? That's where discernment comes into play, what do you truly see, what do you truly know, and what do you truly feel. Fully show up and say, okay, I see it. Where does it come from? How will I allow it to pass through me and give it up on the altar for God to take it off my hands? Responsibility knowing that it's mine, but it can be transmuted into the divine and making amends and adjustments along the way. I'm asking for forgiveness for myself and the other party if needed. Not beating myself up or belittling me. Unfilling my vessel (body), releasing and then refilling through prayer, meditation, chanting, whatever it takes to feel the release and then move onto the next or pause for a bit and let it integrate. We need time to integrate, evolve, and then see the next thing and the next. Not take on all 20 items that will overwhelm you and plunge you into the dark night of the soul. Having full soul awareness and perspective is key.

God is waiting, and your whole collective team is waiting. Are you ready to show up? I'm coming home; I'm coming home, I'm coming home, thank God I'm coming home. Wait, I have always been home, into the light I go, back into me I go. I'm here God, here I AM; there unto me I go, back into the expansive spaciousness of the universe and cosmos. We go back into the comfort of God's love, Jesus's patience, Mary Magdalene, Buddha, Atlantians, all of the ascended masters, my ancestors, and my loved ones. We are all-encompassing, impassioned, passionately me at a soul level. No more confrontation. There is no confrontation. It was my inner conflict. I pull an Oracle card for myself every day. The last two days, I have pulled new beginnings (Cacoxenite) from Crystal Reading Cards (Rachelle Charman), interesting and a big message. Awakening new opportunities, especially on the spiritual path, is a great ally for energy healers because it shares its powerful medicine of awakening the soul. It helps to let go of stale energy and experiences and allows for the fresh, vibrant energy of new beginnings. These are the blessings of new beginnings. This is a time of blessings of rebirth and rejuvenation in every aspect of your life. I'm looking to align with new opportunities that the universe has to offer. I guess what I'm saying is love yourself first completely, and then find that relationship in others. Not codependent, not looking for your next fix, because you are the fix already.

The SOUL mate, no twin flame, twin soul, soul mate need apply here. It already is applied. It is you. You are it. It is God. God is in everything we see, know, feel and touch. All of our senses are on fire, alive, awakened to the whole beingness and oneness which is you. I'm writing this chapter in 2021. In fact, it's March 30. We are still in Covid. Why do I struggle writing this book? Is it my self worth? Is it procrastination? Is it a distraction, or is it the intuitive knowingness that I want to somehow document my experience with Covid? This plandemic, I truly believe it is, that's my knowledge, I hope to God I'm wrong, even my ego agrees. The ego would never bow down in defeat or agreement that would imply that it was wrong. But see what happened there. It has nothing to do with right or wrong. It's about connection and staying connected to God, self, and others. We all have a basic human right to our opinion, beliefs, morals, and ethics. When we split the narrative, we keep scores, push our sides and agendas that get us into trouble. So, remember to breathe, take a step back, evaluate if this is yours? If not, let it go. If it is, then look into it and ask the mother to come in to assist. Watch out if you find yourself sinking, ask for help, reach out, reach up, and know when you surrender to the divinity of who you are. You are being met at that very place of new beginnings. My next book is about how to open up to intuition through my one on one mentorship course *Unleash Your Magic Intuitive Development,* which leads into *Unleash Your Souls Purpose* — that is why we're here.

If you have life, you have purpose. I truly believe that, truly, wholeheartedly believe that. You are ready for new beginnings. This I know to be true. I wholeheartedly want to see you on the other side, whichever side that is for you. I'm ready to see you transform and emerge from the chrysalis cocoon goo and spread your angel wings. You are made for so much more; I mean, God thought you were a perfect creation, right? So, get that through your narrow-minded thick skulls, stop being so HU-MAN, so stuck, so limited. You are divine unlimited pure love consciousness created from source, the very source, the divine spark poof! As I sit here watching the beautiful sunrise upon the ocean, so blessed to be able to do this. That is why I moved out here. The ocean is all about emotion. I feel I have some more emotional releases to go. Letting go of my co-dependency on others, I seem to hold onto people and then detach and let them go without care. I'm not sure why I go to extremes. Slowly, I'm finding out. Listening to the ocean waves and salty air breezes remind me to feel everything because it will be a distant memory one day. Memories are snapshots of our moments to moments, don't disregard any moment. They are all significant. I have a big heart, and I care. I empathize. I guess I work on boundaries more and writing out a personal mission statement of who I am and what I'm about, what kind of people I want to have in my life. There I can see it every day. It's a reminder of why I'm here and what my mission is in life. Guided by God, the universe, by my collective team of angels, guides, and loved ones.

I feel I'm struggling to write, and I feel so disconnected right now. Why am I pushing myself? I feel it's a soul calling, a burning desire to complete my soul's destiny, mission, purpose, and contract. I'm not just filling this space with words but pouring out my heart and soul. Putting it on paper helps me get it out and make the connections back to my heart, back to my soul. A soul's remembrance, you could say, it's time for me to step out completely. No more hiding in the shadows, time to step out and be me fully and completely, and here's my heart imprint. The Imprint of my forever soul traces to the divine, knowing, hearing, seeing, feeling, and just being.

SOULWORK

I love poetry again! What do I mean? I mean somewhere along the way, I dropped it, lost my passion for it, or was told it was silly or not cool.

My good friend Graham Hill reignited my love for poetry through *"Forest of Song,"* a Facebook group. I started small, hung out in poetry groups, and voila, inspiration and magic abound. It made me rediscover things buried from my childhood, things I tucked away.

My challenge to you is to write a short story, a blog, an essay, or a poem. It can be about anything. Just close your eyes, and the first thing that pops into your mind is your HAIKU!

Go for it — I want to hear from you, share them with me here 24khealing@gmail.com.

11

I AM

It's the holiest week of the year, Easter, Palm Sunday, where Jesus rode on a fluffy donkey with beautiful palms laid out before him, better than the red carpet. To Good Friday, where Jesus took the hits for us, entombed in death, we all know death is not final or finite. It is just the beginning. To Easter Sunday, the holiest of days, his resurrection, he rises, we rise, he lives, we live, he is born again, and so are we. Truly imagine the whole scene laid out before you, like a movie in the mind's eye. Even if you are an atheist, do thy not have a heart? Do you not have compassion when someone suffers, is sick, or is dying? Then how can we not see what all this is for?

For all of us to grab a clue (as my mom would say) and stop messing around like we're still in kindergarten, get to the meat and bones of why we're here. If Jesus can start teaching at the age of 12, we can choose to start at any time. To fulfill the contract that we prewrote, prerecorded, and predetermined before we got here only to act like what the hell happened, and why is this happening to me and why why why? So many questions, how about we pick one and start to answer them for ourselves? Stop fucking around; yeah, I said it. Maybe some of you reading this are thinking, wow, she's not messing around, or wow, how rude! I don't care. This is my story, this is my book, and I was preselected to write these words with the hopes that someone gets it, gets inspired, has an epiphany and aha moment, their moment of soul recognition and no ego interference. The ego, you know, is that wall that people feel, that protection system, that part that tells others you are not accessible, ever. I'm here to tell you; you are accessing all of your parts because it's friggin worth it, so are you. You will have moments of sheer wonder and exhilaration, other moments of sheer exhaustion, pain, and madness. Believe me, I have been there, and I'm hugging you and telling you it will be okay. We're all okay, and we're in this together. I will admit, after Shawn Leonard, Aboriginal medium, came on my podcast to tell me to keep writing my book, that spirit is watching, and this is in my soul contract.

It made me feel amazing at first, and then the sneaky ego gets in there and says, oh, you have nothing to talk about, who will read this, and why would anyone bother because no one bothers, and here we go. I was off track for a few days, distracting myself with all the other busyness that one can distract themselves with. Until I decided that I have a voice, I have something to share, and there might be someone who is struggling and thinking no one knows what I'm going through and why am I going through this? Will it ever end? I'm here to tell you it does, it will, and It has. It feels good to write again, gosh, so freeing, like I can feel my angel wings coming, like those baby teeth first cut in, teething pains, growth is temporary pain. Everything in life is temporary, even our meat suits. That's why we're here to walk each other home in the true divinity of God. We are all gods & goddesses. We just forgot. Now we are all waking up slowly. In our soul recognition, we see each other. We remember we are all here together to birth something new, a divine manifestation of pure love. Pure, unconditional love, seeing our souls embrace in one universal hug. The hug of a thousand lifetimes, pure millennia. Am I home? Will I ever be home? What is home? Home is where the heart is. Home is wherever you feel at complete rest and relaxation, to completely let go and be yourself, be free. What is freedom? Freedom to me is self-awareness, full awareness of who I am and that I love who I am, and that's it. Very simple, we tend to over-complicate. Maybe that's my tendency, and I don't want to put everyone in the same box or same group or same category. I know that causes separation.

We need more togetherness and less separateness. I don't want to be the cause or the effect of separateness. I want to be the cause and effect of change, walking fully into our intuitive selves and our soul lifetimes remembrance. Gosh, I make it sound so romantic or of such fantasy and folklore. That's what we need is more fantasy, romance, and folklore, tall tales, imagination. Einstein talks about imagination all the time, now growing up, I thought he was just this giant science guy, but as I soon found out, he is so much more. I was so disconnected from science; to me, it was boring because it was taught from the ego's perspective and not from knowing the soul Einstein is. *He said about imagination, "Logic will get you from A to B, imagination will take you everywhere." "The true sign of intelligence is not knowledge BUT Imagination." "If you want your children to be intelligent, read them fairy tales, and if you want them to be more intelligent, read them more fairy tales."* Gosh, that one so speaks to me because I loved fairy tales as a child, and then around age 10 or 11, I stopped watching, believing, and playing. I even remember telling my sisters it was silly, and it's not real. So sad indeed as I was disconnected, shut off, or shut down from my imagination, trying to retrace the steps back to where this happened and why I stopped believing. Was it a form of protection? A type of fitting in is that when I cover up myself, others won't see me; they always did.

I was 5'11 in Grade 7, blonde, blue eyes, chubby and sensitive — talk about being a magnet for every pain/abuse/trauma/hurt someone had targeted toward me because they saw my heart and how I wanted to "fit in" because I felt I didn't fit in? So, therefore, I pretended to be more mature and more intelligent? How ridiculous is that? I'm having this epiphany while writing this book. I wonder if other authors have the same experiences. As we write, we start to have soul wakeups, soul retrieval, and soul remembrance. Those processes and processed states where one has forgotten through trauma, grief, loss, and some type of pain associated with it. Very interesting indeed, it makes me want to explore this further and continue with my quest. What is the quest? The quest of the Holy Grail, the grail that is in all of us. A sacred grail of light traces of stardust, stars, the cosmos, and our direct connection to the past, the present, and the future. I always knew my strongest ability was Clair-voyance (to see visions, images, a whole movie/play played out before my mind's eye). That's probably why I had so much trouble growing up as a child. I could see people's wounds/hurts/traumas/lies/bullshit. I can see this said grail now before my eyes; it's like a shimmery gold blueprint with star connection points. Maybe these are lifetime points, pivotal moments, like the fork in the road. Where do I go? What do I do? Do I follow my heart? Do I follow my head? Almost like a spider web network or branches spread across a map, a map that is uniquely your own, no one can follow, they might try, but we have free will.

God says that will is mine, so really? I will be the Christ on earth; I AM as God created me; that's a power statement, a statement of fact and truth. The super-power, we all have it. It's there, maybe we forgot about it, no, we dismissed it, and we dismissed ourselves. Knowing fully, we are all God's children in the garden, and we will eat from the tree of knowledge (imagina-tion). I write today 1000 words; yes, 1000 words a day makes me accountable, maybe neurotic or controlling or pushing? Who knows? I'm acknowledging all the thoughts and feelings surrounding this. I know to live fully, we have to let go of control. There is nothing we can control other than how we react to anything. Our reaction is everything. Maybe that's why "resting bitch face" was coined because it was easier to look bitchy than to show any other emotions? I have to control my emotions; therefore, I do not have any emotions? Knowing that emotion is confusing, rather, feelings are accessible. Truly bizarre how I just had this thought pop into my head? Was it mine, or was it in the field? We like to joke about those terms; truly, it's very dismissive, dismissing ourselves through snarky terminology, jokes, and labels. Makes us wonder why we all feel hurt and running with open wounds, trying to fix others and bleeding all over the place. Why not fix our cuts and wounds first, show others how we did this, and collectively heal each other? That sounds like bridging, perfection, a dream I have. That's why I keep writing.

Listening to Billy Joel, one of my favorite singers, *"All About Soul,"* gosh, this speaks to me. *"It's all about joy that comes out of sorrow. Who's standing now, who's standing tomorrow. You've got to be hard, as hard as the rock in that old rock n' roll, that's only part you know in your heart, it's all about soul. It's all about soul. It's all about knowing what someone is feeling, the woman's got soul. The Power of love, the power of healing. You gotta get tough, but that ain't enough, you gotta have soul."* Yes, Billy Joel nailed it, and I'm sure many of you know that many musicians were very spiritual and channeled through their music and lyrics. I think of George Michael, Freddy Mercury, and Prince, Jimmy Hendrix, and so many more. This song really hit me in the feels, crying. There is so much collective trauma, and yes, even out of me. I feel I'm the transmitter, picking up all the debris, thoughts, feelings, and wounds flying into the field. All the wrongs, all the rights, causing separation, the fights, and the makeups. You can't go the distance without too much resistance. I feel so much resistance writing this book. It's like the darkness doesn't want this out. Doesn't want us to heal, doesn't want us to stand in our power, reclaim who we are because we have forgotten who we are. I declare and decree, I'm not playing small anymore, a rapid transformational healer, we all are. I'm tired of the distractions, my distractions from fully stepping into who I am. Who we all are, collectively healing Gaia, Mother Earth, and our divine connection to God and to source, whatever your source is. Your source is all about soul, soul level, soul living, soul inspirations.

So, do you know how powerful and infinite you are? You would be absolutely gobsmacked, I was! That reminds me of my dark night of the soul, the spiritual 2 x 4 to the head, smack and gobsmacked. Then you will smack yourself and say, snap out of it. Why did you wait so long? Why didn't you do this sooner? We were all waiting for you to show up. Like the Messiah, we are the entire Messiah, Jesus calling, walking in thy footsteps. Sometimes meandering off the path, we find our way back and off we go again, every time we double back, in such a rush, a fever rush to thinking we are late, or not arrived. I find myself like that sometimes. That's the ego talking, trying to keep you in a loop. Break the loop and find the circle you want to spiral into, down and up and out into the expansive universe. You can be of service to people and yourself simultaneously, cyclical service for all, for the good of all. And so, it goes, and you're the only one who knows, you and God. What do you choose? I choose life, a life worth living, living to my fullest, most authentic self, the good, the not-so-good, and then there's life. How can one truly live without experiencing what life has to offer? Which, to me, is a rollercoaster. That's how I see it; that's how I know it and feel it. That's my truth. What I wish is for you to find your truth. How you truly feel about yourself and the universe. The universe is waiting, God is waiting, your angels are waiting, your guides are waiting, and your ancestors are waiting. What are you waiting for? The perfect moment, the perfect picture, perfect instructions, there is none; I say just start, just go for it. Freefall into the great unknown, fall, fall, fly, fly, and fly! Let me know how it goes. I'm here to help. I, too, have been there. Spirit casts its net, and you are free!

SOULWORK

Okay, so you made it to the last chapter — time for some fun! Get your crayons, markers, scissors, glue, and gather old cards, postcards, pictures, and magazines. Find a poster board, corkboard, or even a digital board. (trello.ca or canva.com)

Let's create a DREAM VISION board. Think about what your intention, word, or feeling is; what do you want to create for yourself? This is not a goal board, but a dream, a fantasy, a miracle, and this is your miracle year.

Put your word, image, feeling, picture in the middle of the board. Then paste together how that looks and feels Emotionally, Physically, Spiritually, Mentally, Financially, and in Relationships. What do you want to create in each aspect? Choose one or up to three. Otherwise, we get too attached. Add to it slowly, and inspiration will come through all sorts of places, people and dreams. Take your time, no rush, and adjust accordingly, as it might change along the way.

Most of all, have fun. Share your dream vision boards with me through https://www.instagram.com/24khealing.

ABOUT THE AUTHOR

Christine is a Spiritual Medium, Intuitive Energy Coach, Old Soul Healer (empath), Reiki Master/Teacher Animal Communicator, Chaplain, and Soul Purpose Mentor. She resides in Victoria, BC — she is also a bit of a nomad, traveling in her RV across Canada to hold group mediumship events, group mentorship, online training, healings, and coaching.

A lover of Mother and Mother Nature, animals and all beings. She volunteers her time with animal rescues, pet sitting, preserving nature (old growth) preventing homelessness and mental health initiatives, and children. She loves spending her free time in nature, by the ocean, writing, reading, and baking.

You can reach her through all social media channels @24khealing. christine.gold and on YouTube

* 9 7 9 8 5 2 0 2 0 3 6 4 3 *